A Primer for
The Master Genealogist

by

Terry Reigel

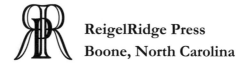
ReigelRidge Press
Boone, North Carolina

The Master Genealogist™ GenBridge™ and Visual Chartform™ are trademarks of Wholly Genes Software, and used by permission.

Second Site and TMG Utility are products of John Cardinal.

Word is a product of Microsoft Corporation.

Microsoft® and Windows® are registered trademarks of Microsoft Corporation.

Adobe® Acrobat® and Reader® are registered trademarks of Adobe Systems Incorporated.

Corel® and WordPerfect® are registered trademarks of Corel Corporation.

Additional copies may be obtained from

Terry Reigel

375 Troy Norris Rd.

Boone, NC 28607

Library of Congress Control Number 2007910138
ISBN 978-0-9801652-0-3

Published for ReigelRidge Press by
Gateway Press, Inc.
3600 Clipper Mill Rd., Suite 260
Baltimore, MD 21211-1953

www.gatewaypress.com

Printed in the United States of America

Contents

Preface

As an avid fan and user of The Master Genealogist, generally referred to as TMG, I have participated in the user-to-user email support list on RootsWeb for some years and in the Wholly Genes Forum since it was introduced. I began posting articles on my *Terry's TMG Tips* website several years ago and there are now over 75 of them. In 2003 I authored two chapters in *Getting the Most Out of The Master Genealogist*, edited by Lee Hoffman.

As I have exchanged notes with new users of TMG on the TMG-List and the Wholly Genes Forum, and talked with them in person at genealogy conferences, it has become apparent to me that there is no resource specifically targeted at helping the new user of TMG. I have observed that many new users would appreciate some assistance in becoming comfortable with a program that is more capable, but also more complex, than their previous genealogy programs. Because of its flexibility, TMG requires users to make decisions about how they enter data in the program. Making choices aligned with one's objectives early can save hours of work that might otherwise be required if one decided to change course later.

This guide is intended to fill that void – provide basic understanding of how TMG works and get new users started on defining just how they can best make use of its capabilities. Some intermediate features are introduced because I believe many new users will want to get started using them. However, this volume does not intend to provide in-depth coverage of the more advanced features. In fact, some advanced features, such as exhibits, styles, language, and the task list, are not addressed at all. There are other resources, some listed in the Appendix A – Other Resources, which provide considerable information on those topics.

Much of the material in this guide is newly written. Some chapters are adapted from articles previously published on my website, rewritten and rearranged to better address the specific needs of the new user of TMG.

This book would not have been possible without the support and encouragement of many people. First, I must acknowledge the continuing support and encouragement of my wife, Nancy, as well as her painstaking reading of the manuscript and many helpful suggestions. Experienced TMG users Virginia Blakelock and Jim Byram encouraged me to undertake the project and provided valuable assistance. Virginia spent weeks carefully proofreading seemingly endless revisions. New user Mark Cunningham reviewed early drafts and provided valuable suggestions in meeting the needs of my target readers. Sue Johnson applied her considerable experience working with new users to help ensure that the explanations are understandable. Judy Madnick suggested many helpful improvements in grammar, punctuation, and wording. Bob Velke provided access to advance copies of TMG and offered advice and support.

Terry Reigel

Boone, North Carolina
December 2007

Introduction

The Master Genealogist is widely seen as the most capable genealogy program on the market. While a few researchers adopt TMG as their first genealogy program, I believe the majority of new TMG users have used one or more other genealogy programs previously. Therefore, this guide addresses what is unique about TMG and what a new user needs to know in order to become comfortable using it and to realize the expected advantages that drove the decision to adopt TMG.

The topics are arranged in an order designed to introduce a new user to TMG in a logical progression. Chapters 1 through 3 lay the foundation, covering TMG's basic concepts, how to get your initial data into TMG, and how to find your way around your data.

I believe it is important to establish some personal standards for data entry in order to provide consistency in your data. Chapter 4 discusses some considerations for arriving at your own standards.

With this foundation, Chapters 5 and 6 discuss the basic data management functions – adding or editing people, events, and sources.

Reports are both research tools and the means for sharing your work. They are covered in Chapters 7 through 9. If sharing your work is important, I suggest you should try some reports early in your data entry process to ensure you are entering the data in a way that produces the output you have in mind.

Chapter 10 provides some guidance in utilizing the many ways TMG offers to customize the program to your needs and preferences.

Chapters 11 through 15 provide an introduction to some of the features that may have attracted you to TMG in the first place – Sentences, Witnesses, Roles, custom Tag Types, and customizing Sources. These tools provide powerful ways to manage your data and to provide the high-quality narrative output for which TMG is known.

Chapter 16 covers Projects and Data Sets, a topic that is important if you are planning on importing additional data into your TMG Project or dividing your data into separate sections. If you are not planning to do either, it can safely be ignored.

A new user will probably want to read through the first few chapters, then take some time to try out TMG's basic features and make some test reports. The more advanced subjects can be explored when you are ready to take them on. It is probably helpful to have a copy of TMG open as you read so you can try out features as you read about them.

TMG offers both "Beginner" and "Advanced" modes of operation. The Beginner mode is intended to provide simpler data entry screens by hiding some more advanced functions. I believe many new users will want to use some of those functions; therefore many of them are discussed in this guide. If you set TMG to Beginner mode when you first opened it, see page 43 for details on switching to the Advanced mode.

The descriptions in this guide include features introduced in version 7 of TMG. If you are using an older version you may find that some of the features described are not available in your version. New features and improvements are frequently added to TMG. If program changes cause information in this guide to become incorrect, updated information will be posted on the updates page on my website: tmg.reigelridge.com/primer

Conventions Used in This Guide

- Terms specific to TMG appear in bold italics at their first appearance and are defined in the following text. Example: *Principal*.

- The names of functions and fields within TMG are always capitalized. Example: Principal.

- The names of buttons appear in a distinctive font. Example: **Save**.

- Menu commands are in the same font and are shown with menu levels separated by angle brackets. Example: **Report > List of ... > People**.

- References to Preferences are shown similarly. Example: **Preferences > Program Options > Data Entry** means that the setting being described appears on the Data Entry page in the Program Options section of the Preferences screen.

  The Preferences screen can be opened with the **File > Preferences** menu command or by right-clicking on many of the windows and choosing **Preferences** from the menu that appears.

- ✔ Tips describing useful techniques that may not be obvious to the new user are marked with this icon.
  TIP

- Like most modern programs, there are usually several ways to accomplish any task in TMG. They often include using a command from the main menu, a Toolbar icon, a keyboard shortcut, and a right-click menu. The text generally describes how to carry out each task using the main menu commands. Where alternate methods exist, they are listed in a sidebar like the one shown to the right. A list of the more commonly used shortcut keys is also found in Appendix B – Shortcut Keys.

Optional Commands
Toggle Primary

Tag box Toolbar:

Shortcut Key: **∗**

- Instructions to use two keyboard keys, such as Ctrl+V, mean you are to press and hold the first key while pressing the second.

- Screenshots were made using the Sample Project that is included with the program, where possible, so readers can find the same screens on their own computers. Other data is used in the screens only where necessary to illustrate specific points.

The Parts of TMG's Standard Screen

● **Menu Bar** – menu commands, like **File > New Project,** are made from this menu.

   ● **Toolbars** – many commands can optionally be made with Toolbar buttons, as described in the "Optional Commands" boxes. The Standard and Layout Toolbars are displayed. See page 89 for more information.

      ● **Details Window** – displays details of the current Focus Person, here displaying the Person View – see next page.

         ● **Children Window** – shows the children of the current Focus Person and their spouses.

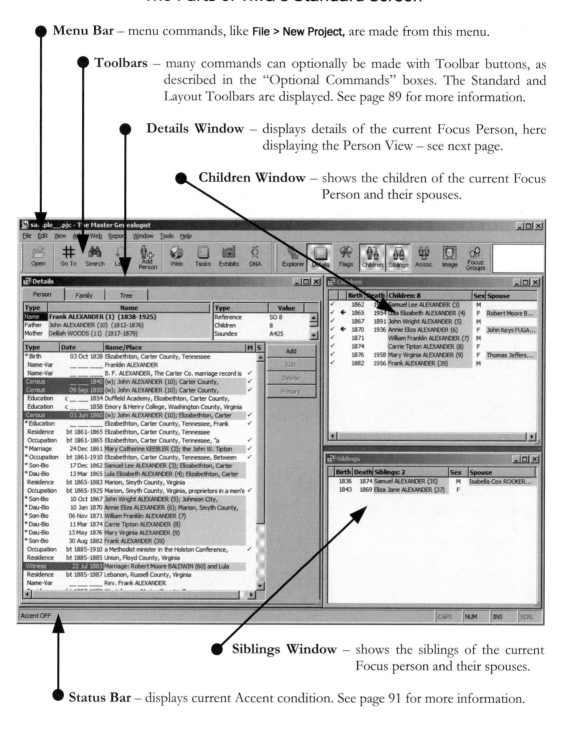

         ● **Siblings Window** – shows the siblings of the current Focus person and their spouses.

● **Status Bar** – displays current Accent condition. See page 91 for more information.

The Details Window offers three views, selected by the tabs at the top:

Person View

See page 2 for more information.

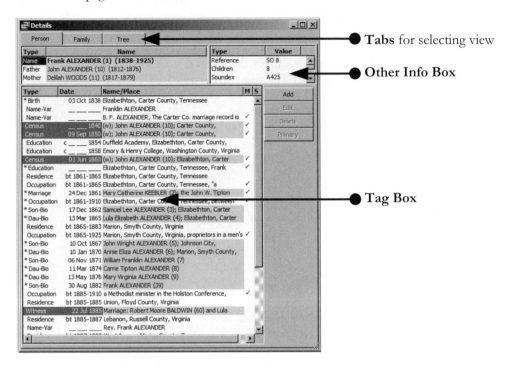

Tabs for selecting view

Other Info Box

Tag Box

Family View

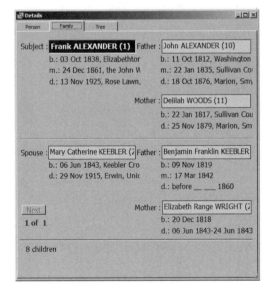

Tree View

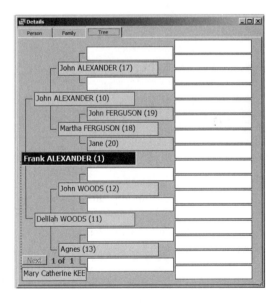

Chapter 1 – Basic Concepts

Congratulations! By adopting The Master Genealogist, you are adding a powerful tool to your genealogy kit. No doubt you are anxious to start experimenting with TMG's many useful capabilities. This primer is designed to help you get off to a good start and then let you explore the more advanced features as you are ready for them.

Before we get started with the nuts and bolts of how to enter your data and produce reports, let's take a few minutes to gain an understanding of some key concepts used in TMG. Understanding these concepts will make it easier to use the program, because the meaning of the windows and screens will be more apparent, and the various features will operate in a more expected way.

If you have used another genealogy program before, you will find that TMG works a bit differently in several aspects. This chapter should help you understand those differences. If TMG is your first genealogy program, you won't have anything to "unlearn," but getting started is still easier with some understanding of these concepts.

Each of the features outlined here will be discussed more fully in later chapters.

Everyone Is a Number

It really helps to grasp this point – every person you enter in TMG is really nothing but a number – an *ID number* to be exact. *Every bit of information you record about that person is in a **Tag** or a **Flag**.* Even the person's name is nothing but a Tag. Birth and death dates and places, marriages, relationships with parents or children – all are recorded in Tags. Simpler bits of information, like the person's sex, are recorded in Flags.

ID numbers are assigned automatically by TMG to each person you add and are the way the program keeps track of everyone. True, everyone has at least one name, but that name can even be blank. Or it may be the same name as several other people in your database.

Some users find it helpful to think of a person entered in TMG as a piece of paper in a ring binder. To start with, the paper is blank except for the ID number written at the top of the page. When we add names or events like birth, marriage, or death, we are adding sticky notes to the page. Those sticky notes represent TMG's Tags and Flags.

All Data is Entered in Tags

As we just saw, Tags define each person's name(s) and relationships with parents and children, as well as events, including birth, marriage, death, and any other events or facts we choose to record. TMG's basic display, the Person View in the Details window, is a list of the Tags for the *Focus Person*. The Focus Person is the person who is currently the subject of the Details window. All the windows, such as Children or Siblings, also refer to that same Focus Person.

The Person View is a list of all the Tags recorded for the Focus Person. The screenshot on the next page illustrates such a listing.

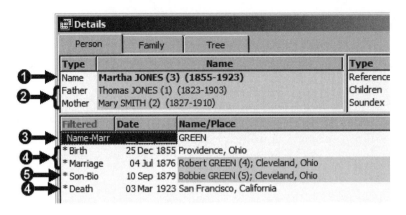

In the upper section of the screen, the labels Name, Father, and Mother are in fact three Tags:

❶ **Primary Name** – the Primary Name Tag for the person. This Tag records the Primary, or main, name of this person.

❷ **Parents** – the two Primary parent/child Relationship Tags that create the links between this person and each of his or her parents.

In the *Tag Box*, or main area, of the Details screen we see all the other Tags recorded for this person:

❸ **Alternate Names** – Tags for any other names by which the person was known. In this case, it is a married name but could also be a nickname or an alternate spelling.

❹ **Events** – Tags for all manner of events can be recorded by Event Tags. Here we have Tags for the person's birth, marriage, and death. We might also have Tags for occupations, anecdotes, military service, or any other event, fact, or note about the person.

❺ **Children** – parent/child Relationship Tags that link this person to his or her children. The Tags for the person's children appear in the Tag Box along with event tags. (In a helpful but sometimes confusing arrangement, the birth date and place shown are from the child's Primary Birth Tag, not from the Relationship Tag).

> Note: The Person View is a *list* of Tags. Unlike some genealogy programs, you do not enter or edit data directly on this screen. You open a Tag Definition screen to do that, as discussed in Chapter 5 – Entering and Editing Data.

Names are Tags

A person may be known by many names. We all have a full formal name, but we often use a briefer version, say with just a middle initial, or even use our middle name instead of our first name. People change their names – after marriage or upon immigrating to a new country, for example – or they may change the spelling.

In TMG you can enter as many of these name variations as you like. Each is entered in a Name Tag. One of those tags is made Primary and appears at the top of the Person View. The name entered in the Primary Name Tag is the name TMG uses by default in many displays and reports.

Events are Tags

Event Tags are used to record the essential genealogical events – birth, baptism, marriage, death, and burial. They are also used for any other kind of event or record we might choose to add about a person. The following list contains a sampling of some standard types of event Tags available in TMG:

Adoption	Census	Engagement	Milit-End
Anecdote	Christning	Graduation	Misc
Annulment	Codicil	Illness	Natlzation
Associatn	Death	Immigratn	Note
Attributes	Descriptn	Living	Occupation
Baptism	Divorce	Marr Bann	Psgr List
Birth	Education	Marr Lic	Residence
BirthIlleg	Emigration	Marriage	Retirement
Burial	Employment	Milit-Beg	Will

Most of these are obviously intended for specific events, but Anecdote, Misc, and Note, for example, could be used for anything for which a specific type of Tag does not exist. Users can also create an unlimited number of custom types to accommodate the kinds of data they encounter.

Most event Tags allow two people to be recorded as ***Principals***. The Principals in a Tag are the two people most closely associated with the event; for example, the husband and wife in a marriage. Being able to enter two Principals is also useful for other types of joint events, like moving or residing at a common address. Additional people can be attached as ***Witnesses***. Witnesses are other people involved in the event.

Relationships are Tags

Perhaps less intuitive, but key to working comfortably with the linkages between parents and their children, is the understanding that these relationships are recorded in Tags. In TMG, a child is linked to each of his or her parents with a Relationship Tag. The Primary Relationship Tags for a person's father and mother appear at the top of the Person View, just below the person's Primary Name.

Since parent/child relationships are simply Tags, correcting relationship errors is simple. For example, if we discover that we have assigned the wrong father to a child, all we need to do to correct that is change the father in the child's Father Tag.

TMG does not explicitly recognize a family as an entity. Rather, the "family" shown in the Family View, a Family Group Sheet, or a Journal report is constructed as needed to display the

Family view, or to create those reports. A couple is displayed as a "family" in the Family View or in reports when there is a Marriage Tag for the two people or when they have children together. Children are included in a "family" based on their Relationship Tags with the parents.

Tag Types and Tag Type Groups

Each Tag created in TMG is of one of the many *Tag Types*. The Type appears in the first column of the screenshot of the Person View on page 2 and provides a label so we know what function the Tag serves. It can be a Name Type, a Father or Mother Relationship Type, or one of the Event Types, like Birth, Marriage, Occupation, etc. The Tag Type controls not only how the Tag functions on the screens, but also defines the default output of the Tag in reports.

Tag Types in TMG are in one of ten *Tag Type Groups*:

- Name
- Relationship
- Birth
- Marriage
- History

- Divorce
- Death
- Burial
- Other Event
- Address

All the Tag Types in each Group behave in the same way. The Name and Relationship (parent/child link) Groups have very special features, as described in the preceding sections. The purpose of the others is obvious from their names, except perhaps the History Group. History Tags are special-purpose Tags for recording events in which a large number of people are involved and are not covered further in this guide.

Perhaps the most significant aspect of Groups is how they constrain changing the Tag Type of existing Tags. Once a Tag is created, it can be changed to a different Tag Type in the same Group. For example, you can change an Anecdote Tag to a Note Tag, because both Tag Types are in the Other Event Group. You can change a Birth Tag to a BirthStill Tag, because both Types are in the Birth Group. Existing Tags *cannot* be changed from a Type in one Group to one in a different Group. If you have an existing Birth Tag, for example, you cannot change it to a Tag Type in the Other Events Group.

Multiple Tags of Same Type Are Allowed

Since all names, events, and parent/child relationships are recorded as Tags, a person can have any number of names, events of each type, and even multiple sets of parents.

The utility of this for names is obvious, as we have already noted. We can record nicknames, spelling variations, married names, and changed names. When we create separate Name Tags for these different names, we can search for a person under any of those names. For example, a married woman can be found under either her maiden name or her married name if both are recorded in Name Tags.

Obviously people can experience some kinds of events multiple times. One might graduate, be married, or be recorded in a census several times. One might have several occupations. While a person may actually be born or die only once, we may have conflicting information about when or where that occurred. We can, if we choose, create multiple Birth or Death Tags, recording in each the information found in one of the several conflicting sources.

In the same vein, we may have conflicting information about the identity of a person's mother or father, or we might choose to record both a person's biological and adoptive parents. In either case, we can create more than one Father and Mother Tag for the person.

Primary and Non-Primary Tags

Closely linked to the concept that a person can have multiple tags of each type is the idea of **Primary** Tags. A Primary Tag is the one Tag of a given type that is used when TMG is required to use just one of them. For example, while a person can have many Name Tags, only one can be at the top of the Person View, at the top of a report, or in a pedigree chart – the Primary Name Tag.

Likewise, while we might enter multiple parent/child Relationship Tags for a person, only one mother and one father can appear at the top of the Person View or on a pedigree chart. Again, those are the parents in the Primary Relationship Tags.

The rules for how many Tags of each Type can be Primary for a person are as follows:

- A person can have one Primary Father Tag and one Primary Mother Tag.

- A person may have one Primary Tag each in the Name Group, Birth Group, and Death Group.

- A person with multiple marriages can have a Primary Tag with each spouse in both the Marriage and Divorce Groups.

- For Tags in the Other Event Group, a person may have one Primary Tag of each Type; that is, one Primary Occupation Tag, one Primary Note Tag, one Primary Residence Tag, etc.

- All Tags in the Other Event Group can have one or two Principals. When a person has several Tags of any Type in that Group, one Tag with each different other Principal can be made Primary. For example, a man might have a Primary Occupation Tag with his father and another Primary Occupation Tag with his son.

- For all Tags that have two Principals, the Primary designation may be assigned differently for each Principal.

Whether a Tag is Primary or not is important in some contexts and unimportant in others:

- The Primary Name Tag appears at the top of the Person View, in the Tree and Family Views, and in the Children, Siblings, and Associates windows. It is used in many reports.

- The Primary Birth Group and Death Group Tags are used to display the life span on various views and charts.

- The Primary Birth Group Tag is used to compute ages at various events.

- Only Primary Marriage Group Tags will be used to display spouses in various screens and reports.

- Certain charts and reports have room for only one Tag of each Type. For example, Pedigree and Descendant Indented Charts can accommodate only one Name, Birth, and Death Tag.

- Most other types of reports can include both Primary and non-Primary Names and events.

When a new Tag is created, it is automatically made Primary unless a previously entered Tag precludes that based on the rules listed on the previous page. You can manually change the Primary status of any Tag by selecting the Tag in the Person View and using the **Edit >** **Toggle Primary** menu command. In the Person View, Primary Tags in the main tag box are marked with an asterisk. In the screenshot on page 2, only the married name Tag – Name-Marr – does not have the Primary mark. All the other Tags in that illustration are Primary.

Optional Commands
Toggle Primary

Tag box Toolbar:

Shortcut Key: *****

Flags

To this point we have discussed Tags, the most commonly used method for recording information. While Tags provide space for recording names, dates, places, memos, and citations, Flags record only a single character of information, for example Y, N, or ? – representing yes, no, or unknown.

There are seven standard Flags, two of them important to most users:

Flag	Allowable Values	Functions
Sex	?, F, M	Controls whether a child is a "son," "daughter," or "child"; a parent is a "father," "mother," or "parent"; and whether male or female pronouns and Sentence Structures are used in reports.
Living	?, N, Y	Controls the display of the Age in the Other Info box in the upper right corner of the Person View, and optionally controls output of information about living people in reports.

A Flag is said to be "set" to a particular value for each person in your database. For example, one person may have the Sex Flag set to "M" and the Living Flag set to "N," while another person might have the Sex Flag set to "F" and the Living Flag set to "?".

Flags are sometimes set automatically when you enter other data. For instance, the Sex Flag is set automatically when you enter a new person defined as a husband, wife, son, daughter, etc., of the current focus person. The Living Flag is automatically set to "N" when you enter a Death Tag for a person, or enter a Birth Tag with a date indicating the person's age exceeds the assumed maximum life span.

Optional Command
Open Flag Window

Layout Toolbar:

Flags

Flags are displayed in the Flag Window. That window is not displayed in the standard Layout but can be opened by using the **Window > Flags** menu command.

The screenshot on the left shows the Flag Window with the standard Flags displayed. You can change the setting of any Flag by double-clicking on that Flag and then choosing the desired value from the Edit Flag screen that opens.

You can also set a particular Flag for a large group of people, using the List of People report. That is described in Chapter 8 – Reports for Research and Analysis.

In addition to the standard Flags, users can create any number of custom Flags. They are useful in keeping track of the people in your Project with a particular characteristic. For example, you might use them to track which line people belong to, whether they had a particular occupation, or if they were in the military.

Sources and Citations

Working with sources is a two-part process. First, you record information about the source itself – its title or description, what kind of source it is, who created it, etc. This is called defining a Source. Once a Source is defined, you attach it to each Tag for which it provided information. That is called citing the Source, or creating a Citation.

For example, a birth certificate might provide a person's name, date and place of birth, and the names of the parents. You would then cite it in the Name Tag of each parent and of the child, in the parent/child Relationship Tags linking each parent to the child, and in the child's Birth Tag.

TMG does not provide for source citations to a person, as some genealogy programs do. Rather, in TMG all Citations are made to Tags. The idea is that a source does not tell us about a person in general. Instead, it tells us about a specific aspect, such as name, or about events in the person's life. Those aspects or events are recorded in Tags, and therefore Citations are associated with the individual Tags that Source supports.

We might record a man's name, who his parents were, when and where he was born, where he went to school, what occupations he engaged in, whom he married, when and where they were married, who their children were, when and where he died, when and where he was buried, when he wrote a will and what it said, or any of hundreds of other bits of information. Generally one source does not provide all this information. Rather, for a well-researched person, we might consult dozens of different sources, each providing various bits of information about our subject. In order to reflect which information comes from which source, TMG allows us to cite sources in individual Name, Relationship, and Event Tags.

Recording Sources

We define a Source by recording its essential elements. Those elements differ depending on the type of source at hand. Typically they include the name of the person or people who created it; its name or title; if it was published, who published it, where, and when; if not published, where it is found; and if unique, like a family Bible, its provenance, or history. To assist us in identifying which elements to record, TMG recognizes over 100 Source Types, based on published style guides. Each Source Type lists the elements appropriate for that type of Source.

The style guides recommend different formats for describing our sources in the initial footnote, in subsequent footnotes, and in a bibliography. When we create reports that display source information in TMG, *Source Templates* automatically take care of formatting the three kinds of output. The Source Templates are instructions telling TMG how to construct the notes, placing the elements in the proper order, correctly punctuated, with quotation marks and italic type used as appropriate.

Citing Sources

Once we have recorded a Source, we need to tell TMG which information we obtained from that Source. We link the Source with the Tags by adding a Citation to the Source in each of those Tags.

Any number of different Sources can be cited in each Tag. When we first enter a person in our database, we would cite the first Source we use for each Tag we enter for that person. Typically we would later find additional sources supporting the same Tags, so we would then create Source definitions for them and cite them as well.

Chapter 2 – Getting Started

This chapter describes the two ways of getting started with The Master Genealogist – starting with an empty Project and entering data, or importing your data from another genealogy program. The following section describes how to create an empty Project and enter the first few people.

If you are importing from another program, you may want to skip to the sections starting at page 11, which describe the importing process and provide suggestions about clearing up any issues that may result from that process.

Starting Fresh

If you want to start with a "blank slate" and enter your data from the beginning, you create a new Project by starting the program and clicking the **New** button on the "Welcome to The Master Genealogist!" screen. If you already have the Program open, perhaps to the Sample Project, use the **File > New Project** menu command. Either method opens the Create New Projects screen.

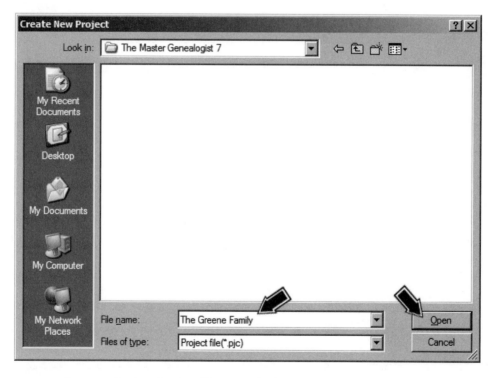

Enter a name for your Project in the File name field, and then click the **Open** button to create the new Project. You are then asked whether you want to use the new Project for an Import or for Data Entry.

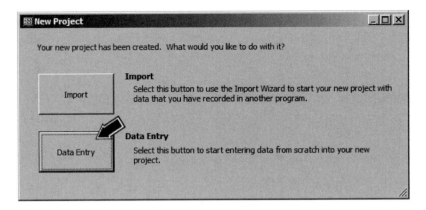

Click on the **Data Entry** button, which opens the New Project Wizard. The wizard is intended to guide you through the process of entering a starting person and his or her parents into your new Project. At Step 1 of the wizard you can click the **Cancel** button if you want to start entering data manually, or click **Next** to proceed with the wizard. At Step 2 of the wizard you enter basic information about the starting person for the Project:

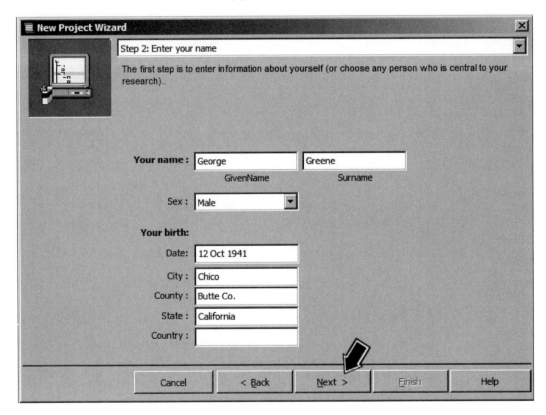

You can start with yourself or another person, leaving blank any fields you wish to omit or for which you do not have information. When you have entered as much information as you like about this person click **Next**. In Steps 3, 4, and 5 enter information about this person's father and mother. At Step 6 add some details about the source of the information you entered. Don't worry about the fine points in any of these steps as you can modify the data entered later if necessary.

When you have finished the New Project Wizard you will see TMG's main screens, which display the information you entered for the starting person. For some tips on navigating to the other people in your Project, see Chapter 3 – Navigating from Person to Person. To add more information to the people you just added or to add new people to the Project see Chapter 5 – Entering and Editing Data.

Importing from Another Program

If you already have your data entered in another genealogy program, or if you have received a file from another researcher that you want to enter into TMG, you can use TMG's Import process to enter that data directly into TMG.

Most genealogy programs, including TMG, can import a GEDCOM file. GEDCOM is a standardized file format created by the Church of Jesus Christ of Latter Day Saints for exchange of basic genealogical data. Because that format was designed to exchange only basic data, use of GEDCOM to export and import may cause the loss of some information. Whether there will be data loss, and the extent of it, depends on the program in which the data was previously recorded, whether that program offered advanced features, and the extent to which the person who recorded the data used those features.

TMG can also directly import from the data files of many common genealogy programs using a proprietary technology called GenBridge™. Use of direct import generally avoids loss of data on import. You should use the direct import method if available for the program from which you are importing, and if you have the files from that program available.

Even if you use a direct import, differences in approaches between TMG and your previous program, along with the methods used to record data in that program, will likely cause some of the imported data to be placed in less than ideal fields. The following sections may help in obtaining the best possible import and offer some tips in approaching the task of cleaning up any remaining issues.

The Import Wizard

Whether you import from a GEDCOM file or directly from another program, you start by choosing Import from the Welcome screen or, if you have a Project open, by using the **File > Import** menu command. Either will open the Import wizard. At Step 1, start with the "Simple Wizard" option and click **Next** to bring up Step 2.

Choose the program from which you are importing, or if you are importing a GEDCOM file, choose that file type as we have in the screenshot on the next page. Enter the file you are importing from either by typing in its name and location or by using the **Locate** button to find the file.

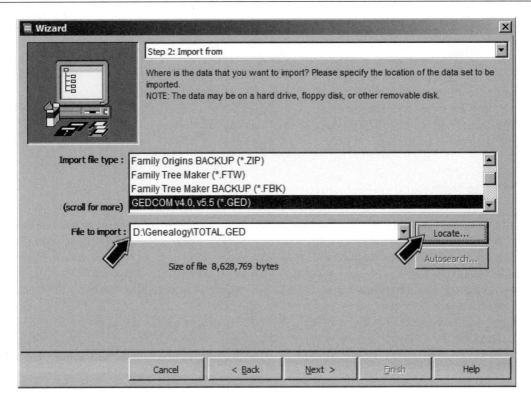

Click **Next** to advance to Step 3:

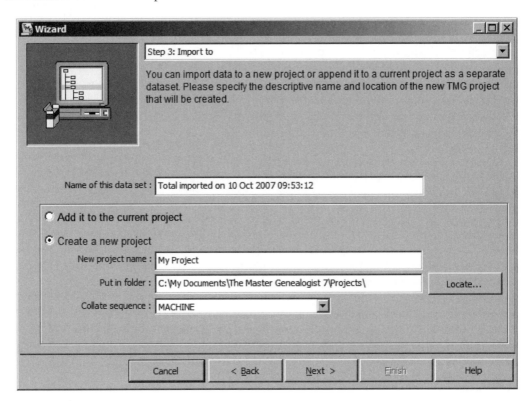

If you have a Project open, you can choose either to add the new data to your current Project or to create a new Project. If you are creating a new Project, as we are above, specify the name of the Project and where it is to be located on your computer, or use the defaults if they are satisfactory. Click **Next** when you are ready to move to the next step.

There may be additional steps in the wizard. The number of steps and options available in those steps depends on which file type you are importing. Generally, the default values for each of the steps are good choices. Continue clicking **Next** as you complete each step until the **Next** button is dimmed, and then click the **Finish** button to complete the import. If you are Importing a large file, the process may take considerable time to complete.

Before investing in any editing of your newly imported data, examine it closely. Make a few sample reports to see how they read. If the results are less than ideal, consider importing again with different settings. The TMG Import Wizard offers many options when importing from most programs. Because of differences between how TMG and your previous program record your data and because of a wide variety of methods employed by users of each program, you may obtain a better import using a different set of options. A little experimentation with different settings may save you hours of cleanup later.

While some options are available with the Simple Wizard, others are available only if you choose the Advanced Wizard at Step 1. For example, if you are importing from a program that combines places and comments in the same field, you may get better results with the Advanced Wizard, which allows you to specify for each item whether that field is more likely to contain a place or a comment.

Cleanup After Import – Places

While the import is likely to bring all the data from the prior program into your TMG Project, significant differences in the way different programs record and organize data may result in some of the information imported being placed in fields where it doesn't really belong. Also, many users find the move to TMG is a good time to correct inconsistent data entry practices that developed over time in their prior program or programs (see Chapter 4 – Personal Data Entry Standards, for some points to consider). In this section we will discuss some strategies for reviewing and relocating data to best take advantage of TMG's capabilities.

Once you are satisfied that you have the best possible import of your data, probably a good place to start the cleanup is with the place names. While many programs provide only a single field for place names, TMG offers ten. Typically, you enter address, city, county, and state each in separate fields in TMG. This allows you to control the output in reports to display the entire place name, or any specific parts of it, to obtain the desired result in any given report.

The Import Wizard will try to place the parts of the imported place name in the correct fields and generally does a good job, particularly for place entries that contain the U.S. state names. The Master Place List offers a powerful tool for correctly aligning misplaced place elements, avoiding having to do so in each Tag individually. Any inconsistency in entering place names – for example, in use of abbreviations, or spelling – can also be corrected in the Master Place List. Changes made in the Master Place List are simultaneously made in every Tag that uses that exact place name, so it is much more efficient to make the changes there rather than in each individual Tag.

Open the Master Place list using the **Tools > Master Place List** menu command, and you see something like the screenshot below.

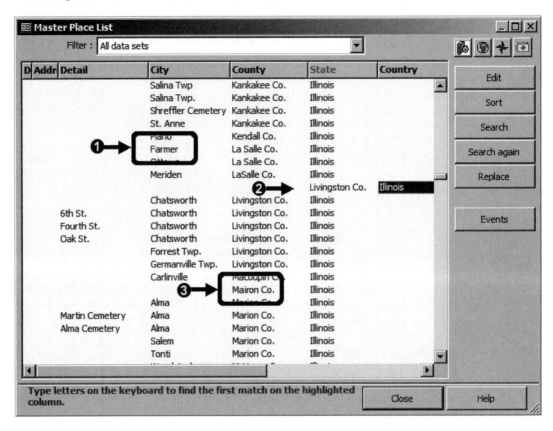

Three common kinds of problems are illustrated above:

❶ **Non-place data** – may be in the Master Place List; for example the occupation "Farmer" here. You can move that data to its proper field with the following steps:

- Select that line and click the **Events** button. The Master Event List opens, displaying only Tags that contain the misplaced information.

- In that list, select one of the Tags and click **Edit** to open the Tag Entry screen for that Tag.

- In that screen, move the information from the Place field to the Memo field, where it likely belongs. You can use the standard Windows functions to cut (the **Edit > Cut** menu command or Ctrl+X keys) and paste (**Edit > Paste** or Ctrl+V keys) to avoid re-typing the data.

Note: After you make the correction, the original entry will remain in the Master Place List until you "optimize" your Project using the **File > Maintenance > Optimize** command on the main menu.

❷ **Misaligned data** – is offset to the right or left of the correct alignment. Here the county and state are offset one column to the right. To correct this, select the rightmost element, and use Ctrl+Left Arrow keys to move all elements to the left. Each element can be moved independently if needed.

❸ **Data errors** – may be present, such as spelling errors or variances from one's personal data standards, like use of abbreviations. Here the name of the county is misspelled. To make these changes, select an element on the desired row and double-click it, or click the **Edit** button to open the Edit Place screen where you can edit any part of the place entry.

Reviewing Sources or People Next

After addressing Places, some users prefer to review Sources next, while others prefer to first go through the people, straightening up Tags and Flags. Sources and Tags may need editing just to print in an acceptable format in reports. Most users will eventually want to review both all Sources and the Tags for each person.

Since these steps require examining every Source or every person in your project, before beginning them you might want to consider whether you prefer to first get everything tidied up using TMG's basic features or whether you want to delay the cleanup process until you have explored some of the more advanced functions and decided which, if any, you want to use.

For example, if you are anxious to use TMG's advanced source-recording features, you may want to examine the alternatives and decide which method best serves your purposes before spending time cleaning up your sources. Likewise if you are eager to use TMG's Witnesses and Roles features to improve how you record wills, census records, and the like, you may want to decide just how you want to use these features before you start to review each person in your Project. Sources, Witnesses, and Roles are discussed in later chapters.

While adopting new features at the same time you are reviewing your imported data may seem more efficient, it may be more comfortable to get your existing data cleaned up before expanding into the more advanced features.

Splitting Large Notes

One common issue is that some programs provide a single large text field in which users record all sorts of notes about a person. Those notes are generally imported into a single Note tag for that person in TMG, with the entire contents placed in the Memo field. This note may include a variety of information, including both information about the person's life and also research notes you may have made. This can result in several issues that can be adjusted to work better in TMG. (Before attempting any of the editing described below, it may be helpful to read Chapter 5 – Entering and Editing Data).

- These entries were often written as complete sentences in the original program. The issue is that TMG's Note Tag is designed to prefix the name of the person or the pronoun "He" or "She" to the Memo contents when creating narrative reports. The result can be something like "He John was raised in a small town..." – the pronoun "He" having been added by the Note Tag's Sentence Structure (see Chapter 11 – Working with Sentences, for more on this). To fix this you can

  - Change the Tag Type from Note to a more specific Tag Type, such as Occupation, Census, or whatever might be appropriate.

  - Edit the Memo to remove the person's name from the text.

  - Transfer date and place information from the Memo to the Date and Place fields.

  If you are otherwise happy with the flow of the note, you could just change the Tag Type to Anecdote, which simply prints the text of the Memo field, and add a Sort Date to sequence the Tag chronologically. (See page 43 to make Sort Dates available if you are using the Beginner Data Entry mode.)

- The Note may cover several separate subjects that may best be broken into two or more separate Tags. Not only does this let you see them correctly sequenced on screen, but it allows you to control which Tags are printed in any specific report, if you use different Tag Types for different types of data. The easiest way to split such Tags is to make copies of the Tag, using the **Add > Copy Tags** menu command. Then for each copy

  - Edit the Memo text, deleting all but the information about a single subject.

  - Change the Tag Type if desired.

  - Transfer the date and place information from the Memo to the Date and Place fields if desired.

  - If the event has no specific date, use the Sort Date to sequence it appropriately with the other Tags.

  - If there are embedded source notes in the text, replace them with regular Source Citations if you wish.

Keeping Track of Who's Been Reviewed

In all likelihood, you will need to eventually review every person in your Project in order to get all the data arranged just as you want it. There is no need to do that all at once. For example, I imported a file of just over 7,000 persons about eight years ago. I've cleaned up people as I work with them or as I create reports that include them, but I have spent more time adding new people or more information about those already entered. As a result, I've added about 9,000 new people, while there are still just under 5,000 from my original import yet to be attended to – you don't have to do it all at once.

Obviously, if you are going to do this review over an extended period, you need some way to keep track of which people you have reviewed and who is yet to be examined. Many users create a custom Flag to mark those that are finished. You can do that with the following steps:

- Use the **File > Flag Manager** menu command to open the Flag Manager. Click the **Add** button to open the Add New Flag screen.

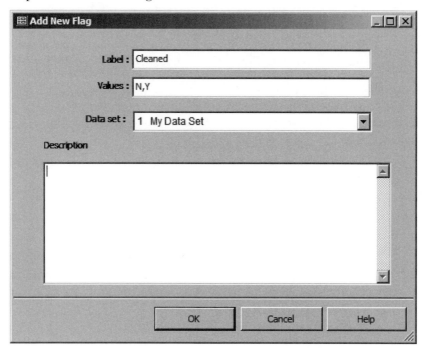

- Give your new Flag a Label, like "Cleaned," and values N,Y (N for "no" and Y for "yes"). By placing N first it becomes the default value, which will be initially assigned to everyone in the Data Set.

- Close Flag Manager, allowing the new Flag to be set for everyone.

- Reopen Flag Manager, select your Cleaned flag, and click **Edit**.

- Change the values to Y,N, reversing the original order. This will not change the values set for the existing people but will make Y the default for any new people you add in the future, who presumably will be "cleaned" as you enter them.

To change the setting of your Cleaned Flag for a person when you are finished with cleanup, double-click on the Flag's name in the Flag Window (see page 7), and then in the Edit Flag window that opens, double-click on the Y value in the column on the left.

Finally, set an Accent color so you can easily see by color coding on any screen who is already cleaned and who is not. See the section starting on page 91 for more on using Accents, including use of the Cleaned Flag in combination with other Accents.

A Cleanup Checklist for Each Person

If you need to review everyone, just what would you want to check for each person? The answer, of course, will depend on exactly how you want to use various TMG features and your personal data entry standards (see Chapter 4 – Personal Data Entry Standards). Every user may have a different list, depending on the user's preferences, the program from which the data was entered, and the methods used in that program. The list below shows the items I check:

- Ensure the Name is entered according to my standards (mixed case, unknown names left blank, nicknames in a separate Tag, common titles and suffixes abbreviated).

- Assign Sureties to every Citation. (Sureties are described on page 54.)

- Add Citations for Relationship Tags with parents, and verify that Sources are cited for all other Tags.

- Add Sort Dates to undated Tags so they are correctly sorted.

- Verify that the Living Flag and my several custom Flags are correctly set.

- Add a Married Name tag for married women so they can be found by that name.

- When multiple items appear in a single Tag, separate them into appropriate Tags.

- Change any source notes embedded as text in Tag Memos to proper Citations.

- Examine "double date" entries and verify that the date was correctly entered, if possible. (Double dates refer to the notation used to account for the shift from the Julian to Gregorian calendars, which various genealogy programs handle differently.)

Use John Cardinal's TMG Utility

John Cardinal, an experienced TMG user, has written a program designed to make mass changes in specific TMG data fields. The program was originally designed to aid in data clean-up after importing and has many functions useful in that task. To mention but three of many examples, it can change names from all upper case to proper mixed-case spelling, change the Living Flag for many long-dead ancestors to N, and find and replace a specified string in any field.

See John's website at **www.johncardinal.com** for details.

Chapter 3 – Navigating from Person to Person

TMG's main screen is made up of a number of individual windows, as shown in The Parts of TMG's Standard Screen, page xi. At any one time all the windows focus on a particular person, called the Focus Person. The Details window displays the events in that person's life, the person's spouse and the parents of both, or the person's ancestors, depending on whether we have selected the Person, Family, or Tree tab. Other windows show the children of the Focus Person, that person's siblings or associates, and Flags set for the Focus Person. Which windows appear depend on the Layout you select, as described in Chapter 10 – Customizing Your Workspace.

Once we have a few people entered in our Project, we want to be able to "navigate" from one person to another to see what is recorded about a person, to add new information, or to add a parent, child, or spouse. TMG offers a number of different ways to move from one person to another, as described in this chapter.

For those who prefer use of the Keyboard, see Appendix B – Shortcut Keys for a list of keyboard shortcuts to perform many of the functions described below.

Double-Clicking a Name

One of the easiest ways to move to another person is to find his or her name in one of the windows in view and simply double-click on the name. The Focus Person is changed to the person whose name you double-clicked.

> Note: If you have "Item Tips" turned on to display additional details about a person or Tag in a pop-up box, that box may appear as you try to double-click on the person's name. If that happens, click once to dismiss the pop-up box, and when it disappears, double-click on the name.

Last Viewed Person Button

We often need to return to the Focus Person we most recently viewed. The simplest way to do that is to click on the **Last** button on the Standard Toolbar. Focus is immediately returned to the previously viewed person.

Go To Button

If you recall the ID number of the person you want to navigate to, you can click the **Go To** button on the Standard Toolbar. When the Search by ID screen opens, type in that person's ID number and click **OK**. Focus will then change to that person.

View Menu

At the bottom of the **View** menu is a list of the ten people you have most recently viewed, as can be seen in the screenshot at the right. You can return to any of them by selecting a name, which returns focus to that person.

The Picklist

The *Picklist* is one of TMG's handier tools for finding people. The Picklist shows not only the names of people but also their ID number, birth and death dates, and the ID numbers of their parents, as illustrated in the screenshot on the facing page. This additional information makes it easier to identify the desired person if there are several people with similar names.

You open the Picklist with the F2 key or by clicking the **Search** button on the Standard Toolbar.

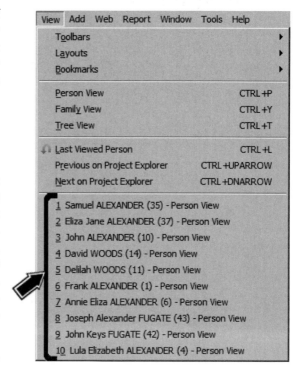

The Picklist is not actually a list of people, but rather a list of names. That means that if a person has several names, say nicknames, a married name, or names with spelling variations, you can locate that person under any of these names. This is a good reason to enter married names, even if you don't intend to include them in any reports, as it is often useful to be able to find a person by married name when you can't recall the birth name. In the screenshot on the opposite page, note that the name selected – Alexander, Isabella Cox – does not have an asterisk in the first column, denoting that is not a Primary name. That is because it is the married name for Isabella Cox Rooker.

To change focus to a person found in the Picklist, you double-click the name or select the name and click the **Select** button.

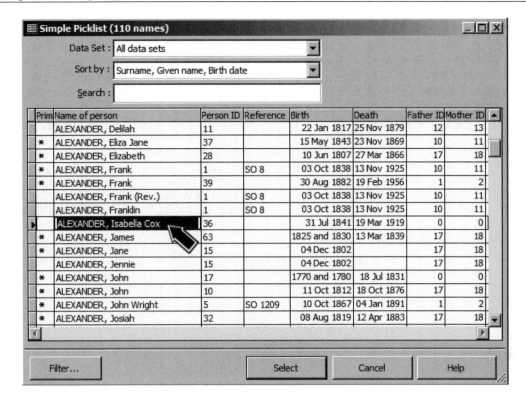

Project Explorer

The **Project Explorer** is another useful tool for examining the people in your project and for navigating between them. It displays people in a very different arrangement than that used in the Picklist. While the Picklist is an alphabetical list of names, the Project Explorer uses a tree-like layout, with people arranged according to their relationships. You open the Project Explorer with the **Window > Project Explorer** menu command.

> Optional Command
> **Open Project Explorer**
>
> Layout Toolbar:
>
> Explorer

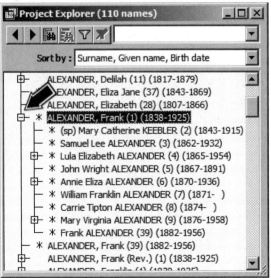

The Project Explorer screen displays each person's name, and if that person was married or had children, a small box with a plus sign appears before their name. Click that box to expand the view to include the spouse and children. In the screenshot on the left, the box in front of Frank Alexander's name has been clicked, and the icon in the box has changed from a plus sign to a minus sign, indicating that his family is being displayed. His wife appears first, followed by his children. Several of them also have boxes with plus signs in front of their names, indicating that they also have families that could be displayed.

Clicking on any of the names in the Project Explorer changes the focus of the other windows to that person. If that doesn't work when you try it, that is because the Project Explorer is not "linked." To link it, right-click on the Project Explorer window and choose **Link Project Explorer to Other Windows** from the pop-up menu.

If you like, you can keep the Project Explorer open permanently by arranging the various windows on your screen to make room for it and saving the Layout, as discussed in Chapter 10 – Customizing Your Workspace.

A useful feature of both the Project Explorer and the Picklist is that they can be sorted and filtered in various ways to display only a limited group of people you might be interested in examining. See page 61 for information on using Filters.

Focus Group

If you are doing some work with a small group of people that will require you to navigate among the members of that group, collecting them in a *Focus Group* creates an easy way to move between them. A Focus Group is simply a group of People in your Project that you assemble for a particular task.

The idea of the Focus Group is to place in the Group a set of people you are interested in examining. Once you have collected the people you want in the Focus Group, you can make any of them the Focus Person of the other windows by double-clicking on that person's name in the Focus Group.

You open the Focus Group with the **Window > Focus Group** menu command. When you open the Focus Group window the first time it will be empty. After that it may contain the people from the previous Focus Group you created. To remove those people, click the **Remove All** button.

The easiest way to add an individual to a Focus Group is to right-click on that person's name in the Details, Children, Siblings, or Associates windows or in the Project Explorer. Then choose **Add this person to the Focus Group** from the pop-up menu. You can continue to add others one at a time the same way, but it is usually easier to use the Add Others tools to add groups of related people. The following example illustrates how these tools work.

In the example, we are creating a Focus Group consisting of Frank Alexander, his wife, and their children. We start by finding Frank's name in one of the screens and adding him to the Group as just described.

Optional Command
Open Focus Group

Layout Toolbar:

Focus
Groups

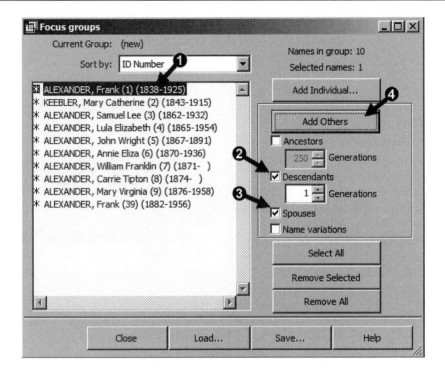

We then add his wife and children by the following steps:

❶ Click once on his name to select him.

❷ Check the Descendants box and set the Generations counter to 1, because we only wanted his children and not any other descendants.

❸ Check the Spouses box.

❹ Click the **Add Others** button.

Note that checking Spouses did not add the spouses of his children. That is because the Add Others function applies only to the people already in the Focus Group, and only to those people there that you have selected. If we wanted to add the spouses of his children, we would now click the **Select All** button to select the children, check the Spouses box, and click **Add Others** once more.

You can save a Focus Group for later use with the **Save** button on the Focus Group screen – enter a name for your group in the New Group Name field in the Save Group screen that opens, and click the **Add** button. Any number of different groups can be saved. To recall a previously saved group, use the **Load** button.

If you like, you can keep the Focus Group open permanently by arranging the various windows on your screen to make room for it and saving the Layout, as discussed in Chapter 10 – Customizing Your Workspace.

TIP   In addition to serving as a navigation tool, the Focus Group is very useful for collecting a selected group of people to be included in various reports, as described in Chapter 7 – Setting Up Reports, or to Export a specific group of people to a GEDCOM file to send to another researcher or to post on a website.

Bookmarks

If you find yourself frequently returning to the same person, the ***Bookmark*** feature may help. A Bookmark functions essentially like a bookmark in a book – it is an easy way to return to the same person.

You can set Bookmarks for any number of people and then easily make them the current Focus Person by choosing that Bookmark. The easiest way to work with Bookmarks is to open the Bookmark Toolbar, which is not open by default. Do that with **View > Toolbars > Bookmark** menu command, or by right-clicking on any open Toolbar and choosing **Bookmark**.

To set a Bookmark for a person, navigate to that person and click the **Bookmark** button on the left end of the Bookmark Toolbar. To navigate to a Bookmarked person, click the drop-down arrow on the left end of the Bookmark Toolbar and select the desired person from the list.

If you like, you can keep Bookmark Toolbar open permanently by arranging it on your screen as you like and saving the Layout, as discussed in Chapter 10 – Customizing Your Workspace.

Chapter 4 – Personal Data Entry Standards

There is no set way to enter most data in TMG. This of course means that the program accommodates a wide variety of users with different needs. The opposite side of this flexibility is that users need to decide on the standards that best meet their own needs and preferences.

This chapter lists some areas in which a user might choose to establish personal data entry standards and discusses some considerations that may be helpful at arriving at those standards.

Your Objectives are Key

Before we discuss specific standards that might be useful, it is helpful to think a moment about your objectives in using TMG. In my view, the single most significant consideration in deciding how to use many of TMG's features is how they can serve your objectives. With your objectives clearly in mind, many of the individual decisions become clear.

For example, some users have a strong focus on using TMG as a research tool. It is important to them to have all the evidence they have found in clear sight as they view it on their computer screen. They also want to be sure that data is entered so it can be easily found with TMG's powerful filter and reporting tools.

Other users might be more focused on arranging their data so it can be output in a way that it can be easily shared with others. Clear display of all the details found in research might be less important than smoothly reading narrative reports that will be enjoyed by relatives sharing the same ancestors.

Still others may be concerned primarily with carefully documenting their findings in order to pass them on to others interested in the same lines. Carefully crafted prose might be less important than arranging the evidence in a way that allows the knowledgeable reader to follow the research and evaluate it deliberately.

TMG can certainly support any of these areas of focus. The most satisfactory results are likely to be obtained if one decides on methods of data entry that best support his or her objectives and then uses them consistently.

Name Conventions

Perhaps the first question in the use of names is to decide which of a person's names to enter, and which to make the Primary name (the one that appears at the top of the Person View and in many reports). As we have seen, TMG allows you to enter any number of names for a person, but only one can be Primary. Traditionally, genealogists have used a person's birth name consistently for all references to that person throughout his or her life. Accordingly, many TMG users try to identify each person's name as given at birth and make that the Primary name. However, some people use their middle names exclusively, or change their names entirely. In such cases, current relatives may not even recognize the birth name, so some users prefer to make the more commonly used name Primary.

Most people don't actually use their full birth names in everyday life. They use some combination of names and initials or a nickname. Should those names be entered in TMG? You should enter them if you want them to be mentioned in reports, as "He was known to family as Bobbie." Likewise, you would if you wanted a name other than the primary name to be used in narratives (see Name Variations in the discussion of Advanced Data Entry beginning on page 43). Otherwise, entering them is totally optional. My practice is to enter the full birth name and ignore the various combinations of names and initials. When a person consistently used only a middle name I do create an additional Name Tag reflecting that information. I ignore nicknames that are obvious diminutives of a given name, such as Johnnie for John.

Many people actually change their names, especially surnames. The most common example is taking a spouse's surname at marriage. Others changed their names when they immigrated to another country. Entering these additional names makes it easier to find the person in the Picklist or Project Explorer, whether or not you intend to include them in reports.

Finally, we have many cases where surnames, especially, are found with many different spellings. Commonly, the spelling evolved over generations. In earlier times little attention was paid to spelling, so many variations can be found. Other disparities are simply errors made by record-keepers. Which, if any, of these should one record? Some users like to record every variation found. My preference is to record the most commonly used spelling, preferably the one most used by the person involved, when it is possible to determine that.

In the case of a surname that changed over time, I try to use the spelling actually used by each generation. Then, for convenience, I add a "standard name" tag, using the current spelling, so I can find a member of the family without having to recall which spelling was used by a particular individual. I never include that standard name tag in any reports.

In addition to the name itself, one has to decide whether to include titles such as Dr., or military rank, and suffixes such as Sr. or Jr. Except for the last, these are obviously not part of one's birth name. Still, in an exception to the practice of using birth names as a primary name, many users add those titles when they were commonly used by the person in adult life.

Place Conventions

There are several issues around the recording of place names. The first is the fact that the names of many places have changed over time. This is true occasionally for towns and cities, but more often county, state, or country boundaries changed so that a given town found itself in a different county, state, or country. Many genealogists recommend that one record a place name as it was used at the time of the event being recorded. An advantage of this approach is that the place recorded in the event Tag suggests where supporting records might be found.

Following this convention, however, can produce a series of Tags recording events that occurred in the same place but appear to have been in different places because the names are different. One way of dealing with this is to add notes, perhaps in the Memo field of one of the Tags, noting the change of the place name.

Another aspect of recording place names is to decide which place levels – Detail, City, County, State, Country – to enter. Some favor entering only the levels found in one's sources so that the Tags reflect what the sources say. Others prefer to enter the full place name when it is known, even if the sources for that event show only a partial name. The trick here is to be sure that the place mentioned in the source really is the one you think it is and not a similarly named place in another county or state.

Related to this is the issue of entering country names. Some users, especially those who think they may share their work with relatives in other countries, prefer to always enter the country. Many others prefer to omit the name of their own country to reduce the large number of repetitions of the country's name in reports.

Abbreviations

Use of abbreviations, especially in names and place names, is an area about which there is considerable disagreement. Some suggest that all abbreviations should be avoided, because they tend to change over time and may become confusing to future readers. Sharing your data with a relative speaking a different language offers further opportunity for confusion.

The standard postal abbreviations seem somewhat appealing, in part because they can shorten long place named in crowded charts. However, experience teaches that they too change over time, and many readers find even the current ones confusing. One way to avoid difficulty with these abbreviations is to spell out the name in full during data entry, then when creating a report in which space is tight choose the option to substitute the standard abbreviations on the Places tab of report Options.

My practice is to limit use of abbreviations to a short list – certain titles, like Dr. and Capt., and in place names St. and Ave. for street and avenue, Twp. for township, and Co. for County.

Conflicting Data

We often find conflicting information about the dates or places that events occurred, particularly with births, marriages, and deaths, in my experience. As described in Chapter 1 – Basic Concepts, TMG allows one to enter an unlimited number of Tags to record these events. So the straightforward way to record conflicting information would seem to be to simply enter a new Tag for each new date or place found. Whether this is a good approach depends largely on your personal objectives.

If your priority is to have all the available data clearly visible, creating multiple Tags is a good way to do that. But this approach creates a rather disjointed and confusing report, perhaps like

> She was born 25 Jan 1853 in Johnson City. She was born 25 Jan 1854 in Johnson City. She was born 28 Jun 1854 in Rush Creek.

If keeping the conflicting data visible is a priority, one way to do that, while making your reports seem more sensible and also providing a way to communicate what you think is the most likely information, is to create "alt" Tags. These are custom versions of the standard Birth, Marriage, and Death Tags and are used for the "alternative" data you have found. With such Tags your output might read something like

> She was born 25 Jan 1854 in Johnson City. She has also been reported to have
> been born 25 Jan 1853 in Johnson City. She has also been reported to have been
> born 28 Jun 1854 in Rush Creek.

However, if smoothly reading output is a priority you might create only a single Tag using the information you consider most likely. Then either note the conflicting information in the Tag Memo or "bury" it in the Citation Details of your Citations. This way, the casual reader sees only the more likely version, while a more serious reader can still see the conflicting data.

In practice, I find "alt" Tags more useful in the early stages of research on a line. Often the conflicts can be resolved during the course of research, and I end up removing the "alt" Tags and rolling all the versions into a single Tag with the differences recorded only in the Citations.

Multiple Persons in an Event

In Chapter 1 – Basic Concepts, we saw that most Tags can have two Principals. This is obviously required in such "couples" events as engagement, marriage, and divorce but is useful in many other contexts as well, such as two parties buying and selling land. Many events include whole families or even groups of unrelated people. A family's enumeration in a census, move to a new city, or immigration to a new country are common examples of where this occurs. Entering the additional people as Witnesses makes it easier to see that the whole family or group was involved in the event. It is also easy to include mention of other participants in narrative reports if they are all included in the same Tag.

See Chapter 11 – Working with Sentences and Chapter 12 – Witnesses for details on how to effectively use the capability to enter multiple people in a single Tag. Also see the following section for some cautions if the ability to export to a GEDCOM file is important to you.

Is GEDCOM Export Required?

As mentioned in Chapter 2 – Getting Started, the GEDCOM standard is the only generally accepted way to exchange genealogical data, and the only format accepted by most genealogy programs and websites. It was designed to exchange basic data, not the more complex information that advanced programs like TMG can record. If exporting your data to GEDCOM is important, you need to carefully consider how you enter data in TMG. Basic names, birth, marriage, death, and burial data will export without issue. Other data must be entered with care if it is to be exported. For example, GEDCOM allows only specific two-person tags, and the two people must be in a "family" – that is, be married or have children together. So a census Tag with a husband and wife as Principals is recognized, but a land sale Tag with two unrelated Principals would not be.

The GEDCOM standard has no provision for Witnesses, so, for example, children entered in their parents' census Tag as witnesses will leave no record of their being in a census in the exported data. Each child would need a separate census Tag if that information is to be exported. Source data is exported, but not TMG's Source Templates. So the exported source information may not be easy to reconstruct in a coherent form.

If you must export beyond basic data by use of GEDCOM files you must enter your data very carefully. Experiment with small samples, or consult the available references to ensure that what is important to you can be included in the export.

Many users find the TMG features which are not supported by GEDCOM so compelling that they elect to forgo the ability for a complete export and instead share their data by TMG's reports and websites created by John Cardinal's Second Site program (see Chapter 9 – Genealogy Reports).

Source Conventions

It is easy to accumulate dozens, or even hundreds, of Sources in the Master Source List. They quickly become too numerous to easily find a particular one in the list. Many users devise a code system for the Abbreviation field in the Source Definition to organize the list in a more manageable way. For example, the following are some of the codes I use.

Code	For	Code	For
bapt-	baptism record	bur-	burial record
Bible-	family Bible	cen1810-	1810 census
birth cert-	birth certificate	ltr-	letter
bk-	book	man-	manuscript

Following the code, I add the name of the individual for records about a specific person, the title of the item if it has one, or a short description. For a census I add the state and county. By using such codes and then using the "Less" mode of the Master Source List (see page 49), the sources are organized by type. Deciding on a system that suits your own needs early in the data cleanup may be helpful.

A more fundamental issue is to decide exactly the level of detail you wish to include in each Source you define. For example, one might create a single Source definition for all birth certificates. Or one might create a single Source for all birth certificates issued in a single county or state. Or one might create an individual Source for each certificate.

Defining fewer Sources does not necessarily mean that less detail is actually included in the finished footnotes. It just means that instead of recording the details – like the name of the person, issue date, and certificate number – in the Source, you would record it in the Citation Detail when you cite the source. The result is fewer Sources listed in the Master Source List but the need to enter more details each time the Source is cited. For those who care about formatting the footnotes according to the recommendations of style guides, it is more difficult to obtain the suggested order of terms when using more broadly defined Sources.

You may see the terms "Lumper" and "Splitter" used as shortcuts to describe these two approaches. A Lumper would define one or a few Sources in TMG for each type of source, while a Splitter would create a separate Source in TMG for each separate record. The default Source Types are designed to work as a Splitter would use them. If details are to be shifted to the Citation, as a Lumper would, some editing of the Source Templates will be required (see Chapter 15 – Customizing Sources).

By using a coding system for Source Abbreviations as described above, a large number of Sources can be easily managed, so the decision between lumping and splitting is largely a matter of personal preference. In practice, most users probably "lump" some types of sources and "split" others. The most important point may well be to be aware of the choice and to make sure that your Source definitions and Citations are entered so that all the needed detail is included in one or the other for each Citation.

Create a Test Project

A good way to try out alternate approaches safely is to create a test Project. You can then use that Project to try out various ideas and find those that work best for you without worrying about possibly messing up your real data. Some users like to construct a simple Project with a few well-known people for this purpose, but I prefer to make a copy of my real Project so I can explore alternate methods with the data I will actually use. Just be sure to give the copy a distinctive title so you don't accidentally start entering your "real" data in it.

If after a while the test Project becomes filled with ideas you decided to reject, simply delete it and create a new one, again copying your real data.

Chapter 5 – Entering and Editing Data

TMG offers the user extensive control over almost every aspect of data recording, and the resulting display in screens and output in reports, charts, and websites. This chapter is designed to help users feel more comfortable with the basic tasks of entering and editing data, and with the screens and data fields used for those tasks.

As discussed in Chapter 1, a fundamental concept used in TMG is that virtually all information about each person is entered in Tags. Tags define the person's names, relationships with parents and children, and events, including birth, marriage, death, and any other events or facts we choose to record. In this chapter we see how to create and edit those tags.

We will assume that the reader has either imported data from another genealogy program or has used the New Project wizard to enter basic data about a few people. We will now discuss the next steps a user will want to undertake – editing that data, adding new data, and adding new people.

This chapter consists of four main sections:

- Understanding the three main types of Tag Entry screens. Tag Entry screens are used to enter and edit data in Tags.

    - Name Tags.

    - Relationship Tags.

    - Event Tags.

    Each type has different fields as needed to serve its purpose. We've omitted some more obscure types, such as History tags, which are not generally used by new users.

- Applying this information to

    - Edit existing Tags.

    - Add new Tags for the people already entered.

    - Add new people to the Project.

- Two features that are useful in data entry:

    - A warning when you may have entered a person already present in the Data Set.

    - Tools for repeating data elements previously entered elsewhere.

- Using the Advanced Data Entry Mode. To this point, the discussion uses the Beginner Data Entry mode, which hides some more advanced features to make the screens simpler. The final section discusses use of the Advanced mode.

Name Tags

The Tag Entry screen for Name Tags contains six areas for user input:

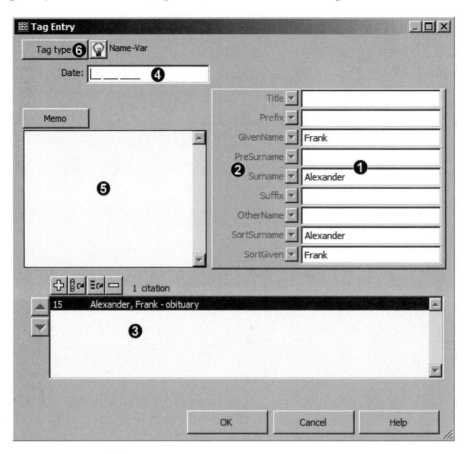

❶ **Name Part fields** – is where the actual name is entered. Only four of these fields are of concern to most users:

- Title – used for titles, such as Dr. or Capt. (you can abbreviate them or not as you prefer).

- GivenName – used for given names, such as John Robert or Sue Ann.

- Surname – used for the person's surname

- Suffix – used for suffixes such as Jr., Sr., or III.

All the other fields are used for advanced features, such as Name Styles or custom sorting of the name in the Picklist and Project Explorer. Consult Help for details on using them.

TIP

Enter names in mixed case, like Jones or McClure. The names can still be displayed in the various windows in all upper case if you prefer, and that is the default setting for surnames. You can change how they are displayed in **Preferences > Current Project Options > General**. Reports also have options to print names in upper case if desired.

❷ **Name Part labels** – are dimmed, indicating they cannot be changed. (Actually, they can be changed by use of Name Styles, but that's an advanced feature not covered here.)

❸ **Citation features** – are covered in Chapter 6 – Working with Sources.

❹ **Date field** – has no meaning for primary names and is generally not used for other names. It can be useful when a name was adopted at a specific date, for example with a legal change of name.

❺ **Memo field** – is generally not used in primary Name Tags, but may be used for name changes, nicknames, etc., to record details about that name.

❻ **Tag Type button** – allows you to change to another Tag Type in the Name Tag Group, for example, to a nickname or married name tag.

Parent/Child Relationship Tags

The Tag Entry screen for parent/child Relationship Tags contains five primary areas for user input:

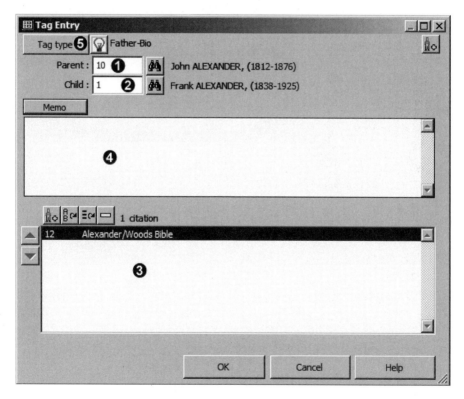

❶ **Parent ID number field** – is for the ID number of the parent in this relationship.

❷ **Child ID number Field** – is for the ID number of the child in this relationship.

Note: To link a child to a different parent, or a parent to a different child, simply change the parent or child ID number to that of the new person.

❸ **Citation features** – are covered in Chapter 6 – Working with Sources.

❹ **Memo field** – is generally not used in Relationship Tags.

❺ **Tag Type button** – allows you to change to another Tag Type in the Relationship Tag Group, for example, to an adopted Relationship Tag.

Event Tags

There are several different groups of Event Tags, including Birth, Marriage, Death, and Other Event. The Other Event group contains types like Occupation, Census, Note, Will, and many more. The example below is for a Marriage Tag. The Tag Entry screen for Event Tags contains seven primary areas for user input:

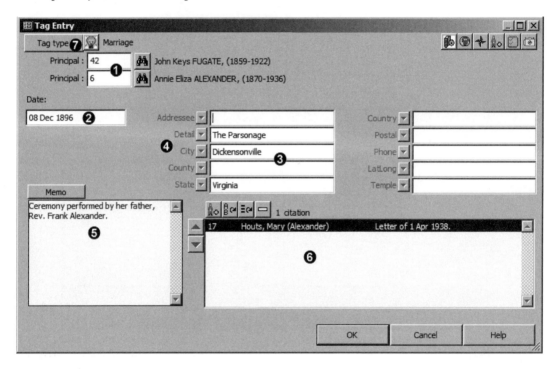

❶ **Principal ID number fields** – contain the ID number(s) of the Principal(s). Most event Tags allow for two Principals, that is, people who participated in the event. Birth and Death Tags allow only one. (Additional participants can be added as "Witnesses" but only in Advanced Data Entry mode, see page 43.)

❷ **Date field** – is where the date of the event is entered.

❸ **Place Part fields** – are for the place where the event occurred. Only five of these fields are of concern to the most users:

  ▪ Detail – used for street address, name of church or cemetery, or similar details.

  ▪ City – used for the town or city.

- County – used for name of the county.

- State – used for the name of the state.

- Country – used for the name of the country.

Any of these fields can be omitted if not known or if the user prefers they not be used. The other fields are for advanced features, such as Place Styles, or for special applications, such as Address Tags and Repository place entries. Consult Help for details.

❹ **Place Part labels** – are dimmed, indicating they cannot be changed. (Actually, they can be changed, by use of Place Styles, but that's an advanced feature not covered here.)

❺ **Memo field** – is used differently for various event Tags. In some cases, such as Birth or Marriage Tags, it may be used to record additional details about the event. In other cases it is used for essential information. For example, in a Note Tag it contains the text of the note, and in an Occupation Tag it would contain the occupation, such as "a bricklayer." The Reminder function, described below, explains how to use it for commonly used Tag Types.

❻ **Citation features** – are covered in Chapter 6 – Working with Sources.

❼ **Tag Type button** – allows you to change to another Tag Type in the same Tag Group. The event groups are Birth, Marriage, Divorce, Death, Burial, and Other Event.

For those who prefer use of the keyboard to the mouse, the F9 key serves the same purpose as the **OK, Close,** or **Select** buttons in virtually all TMG data entry screens.

TIP

Reminder Screens

Many Tag Types have Reminders that provide tips for entering data so that the best results are obtained in reports. The one for the Occupation Tag Type is shown at the right.

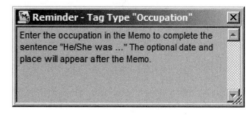

By default, the Reminder screen opens automatically when a Tag Entry screen is opened if the Tag Type has an associated Reminder. That feature can be disabled in **Preferences > Program Options > Data Entry**. Reminders can be turned off or on manually by using the light bulb button that appears next to the **Tag Type** button on the Tag Entry Screen.

Editing Existing Data

To edit any existing data, you edit the Tag in which that data resides. You open the Tag Entry Screen for that Tag by

- Double-clicking on the Tag Label – the word "Name" in the example shown on the next page – or

- Clicking once to select the Tag and then pressing the F5 key on the keyboard, or pressing the Enter key (provided that option is enabled in **Preferences > Program Options > Tag Box**).

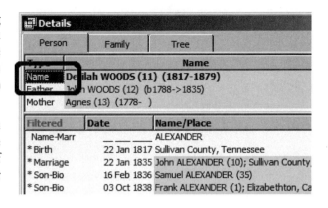

When the Tag Entry screen opens you will see the fields described in the preceding sections. You can edit any of those fields, modifying, deleting, or adding data as you wish.

Adding New Tags to an Existing Person

The first step in adding a new Tag to an existing person is to make that person the focus of the Person View. Then use the **Add > Add Tag** menu command to open the Tag Type List, which is shown below.

Choose a Tag Type that is appropriate for the data to be entered and click the **Select** button, or just double-click the desired Tag Type. This will bring up a Tag Entry screen, as shown in the preceding sections, where you can enter the desired data. In the screenshot we have selected the Baptism Tag Type in order to create a Baptism Tag for our subject.

Optional Commands
Open Tag Type List

Tag Editing Toolbar:

Shortcut Key: **F4**

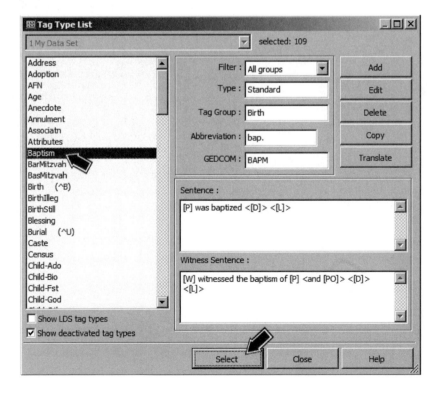

TIP For certain commonly used Tag Types, such as Birth, Marriage, Death, and Burial, you can open the Tag Entry screen directly from the **Add** menu or with a keystroke. The keystrokes are listed after the Tag Type label in the list in the Tag Type List. For example, note in the screenshot on the facing page the "^B" in parentheses after the label "Birth," meaning you use the Ctrl+B keys to open a Birth Tag.

Adding New People

So far we have discussed editing existing Tags and adding new Tags to people already entered in your Project. Now we will cover adding new people to the Project.

If the new person is related to someone already in our Project, we navigate to that person first. Then use the **Add > Add Person** menu command, which will open the Add Person Type screen, in which we specify how the new person is related to the person currently in view on our screen.

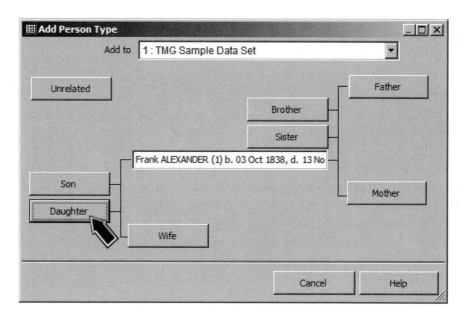

In this case we are going to add a daughter of Frank Alexander, so we click the **Daughter** button.

 TIP For the more common relationships, you can select how the new person is related directly by selecting the relationship from the Add menu.

If the new person is a child of an existing person, as in this case, we are asked to specify who the other parent is on the Select Second Parent screen, as shown on the next page.

This screen lists the spouse(s) of the current person, and generally we just select the correct spouse. We might also select "None" if we don't know who the other parent is or we don't have that parent entered in our Data Set. If the other parent is entered but not listed, we can enter his or her ID number in the field below "Identify another person," or search for him or her with the binoculars button. We click **OK** when we have completed this screen.

We now see the Add Person screen, as shown in the screenshot on the facing page. The Add Person screen is a sort of short-cut screen that allows us to do a number of things from a single screen:

- Have the program assign an ID number to the new person.

- Create a primary Name Tag for the new person.

- If the new person was identified as a parent or child of the current person, create parent/child Relationship Tag(s) to link the new person to the parent or child.

- If the new person was identified as a spouse of the current person, create a Marriage Tag for them.

- Optionally, create Birth and Death Tags for the new person.

In the example illustrated in the screenshot on the facing page we are adding the information we have about a daughter of Frank and Mary Alexander, using information we have found in one of Frank's letters. We have entered the following information:

- Her given name and surname.

- Her date and place of birth.

- Her date and place of death.

- A Citation to the source of our information. (Citations are discussed in Chapter 6 – Working with Sources.)

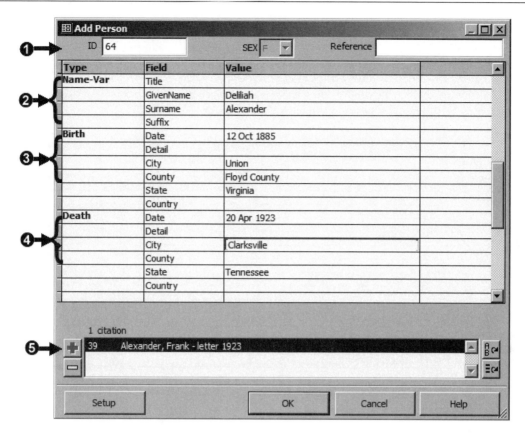

When we click the **OK** button TMG will add the following items to our Data Set, based on the numbered lines in the screenshot:

❶ **ID#** – TMG automatically assigns an ID number for the new person.

❷ **Name Tag** – a Name Tag will be created for the new person.

❸ **Birth Tag** – because we entered a birth date and place, a Birth Tag will be created. Had we not entered anything on these lines, no Birth Tag would be created.

❹ **Death Tag** – because we entered a death date and place, a Death Tag will be created. Had we not entered anything on these lines, no Death Tag would be created.

● **Marriage Tag** – had we said the new person was a spouse of the current person, a Marriage Tag would have been created, regardless of whether or not we entered any date or place information. Because in this example we said the new person was a daughter, the Marriage Tag lines do not appear. Caution: depending on the size of your Add Person screen, you may have to scroll down to see the Marriage Tag lines.

❺ **Source Citation** – will be added to each Tag created. Only a single Source may be cited in the Add Person screen, and that Source will be cited in every Tag created.

The new person will become the Focus Person when the Add Person screen is closed. You can then add other Tags if you like, or edit any that were added by the Add Person screen.

Duplicate Person Warning

If you are entering people from an extended family, it is quite possible not to recognize a newly found relative as someone you have already entered in your Project. As you enter new people, TMG compares them with people already in your Project and warns you if the person being entered may be the same as someone already in the Project:

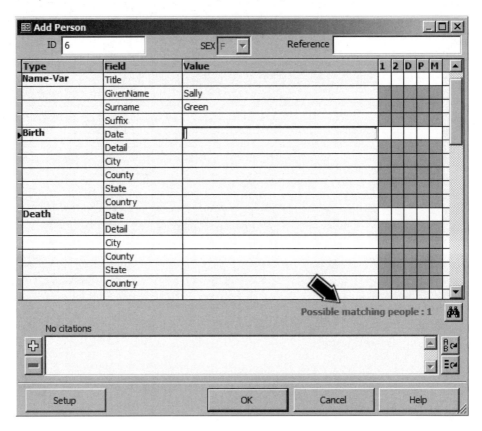

When you have entered enough information for TMG to tentatively identify a duplicate, a warning appears in red, as marked by the arrow above. The binoculars (search) button appears next to the warning so you can check the possible duplicates. If you click that button the Picklist appears, displaying only the potentially matching person or persons. If you decide the new person really is a duplicate, you can use the **Cancel** button to exit the Add Person screen. If it is not, simply continue to enter the new person.

The criteria used to identify potential duplicates are specified in **Preferences > Program Options > New People**, as shown in the screenshot on the facing page.

Uncheck the "Check for duplicates while adding new people" option to turn off the feature. The options shown in the screenshot are the default values. You can adjust any of them to allow less stringent conditions so that less then perfect matches will be identified.

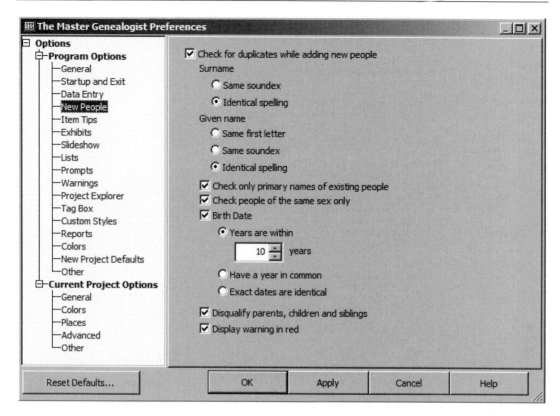

Note: There is a totally separate feature, opened with the **Tools > Check for Duplicate People** menu command. That feature checks all the existing people in your Project for potential duplicates, rather than checking only the new person being added as this feature does.

Entering Repeated Place or Other Data

We often find that we need to enter the same information over and over again, most commonly for place and citation information. TMG offers three tools to make this easier and help avoid spelling errors and inconsistencies. The functions work in almost every data entry field in TMG – try them and I think you will find them most helpful. To use them, place the cursor in the desired field and press the indicated key or keys:

F3 – Repeat Function – recalls the most recently used value in that field. Press again for the next prior value, up to 15 prior values.

Ctrl+F3 – Repeat List – opens a list of up to 15 prior values, from which you can select the desired value. In the screenshot on the next page, we have placed the cursor in the Given Name field in a Name Tag and used the Ctrl+F3 keys to open this Repeat List. We would choose the desired name by double-clicking on it, or by selecting it and clicking the **OK** button.

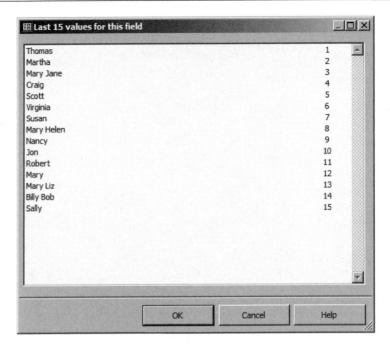

Note: Special rule for citations – the Source number and Citation Detail fields are
recalled together. Using the F3 or Ctrl+F3 keys in either recalls the values for
both. See also the special buttons for repeating Citations on page 52.

F2 – Search Function – opens a list of all values previously used in that field. Once the
list appears, type a few letters of the desired value, and the list will scroll to it:

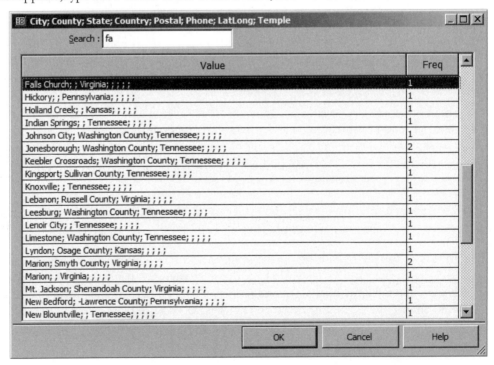

In this example we have placed the cursor in the City field in an event Tag and used the F2 key to open this list. We typed in the letters "fa" in the Search box at the top of the screen, causing the list to scroll to the Falls Church line. We would choose the desired name by double-clicking on it, or by selecting it and clicking the **OK** button.

Note: Special rule for places – place the cursor in the field for the smallest geographic level you want to recall before you press F2. Then when you select your desired value, all higher-ranking places will be filled in as well. In the example above, both the city, Falls Church, and state, Virginia, would be inserted.

TIP   The F3 key provides a very useful way to "copy" source citations from one Tag to another. To use it, open the Citation you wish to copy. Press F9 twice or click the **OK** button to close both the Citation and Tag Entry screens. This saves the Citation information to the "repeat list." Then open the Tag Entry screen for the Tag to which you want to copy the Citation, open a new Citation, and use F3 to recall the data just saved.

Consider Switching to Advanced Data Entry Mode

Several times above we referred to the Advanced Data Entry Mode. The Beginner mode simplifies the data screens by hiding some fields that would appear in Advanced Mode. Here is a Tag Entry screen for a Marriage Tag in Advanced mode:

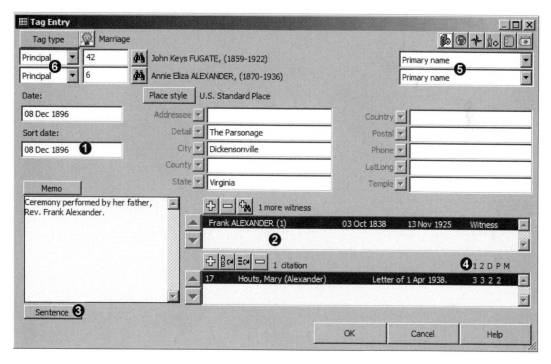

The most useful features available only in Advanced mode are listed on the next page.

❶ Sort Dates – control the sorting of tags in the Details screen and in reports. TMG automatically sorts dated tags in chronological order, but undated tags are sorted to the top or bottom of the list (depending on which you select in **Preferences > Program Options > Tag Box**). Sort Dates, which never appear in any output, allow you to place undated tags in their approximate chronological order, or to place tags in any desired order regardless of the actual date entered.

❷ Witnesses – allows you to enter participants in events beyond the two Principals. Witnesses are useful when you want to record in a single Tag members of a family moving together, members of a household enumerated in a census, various participants in a wedding, and many other examples. Use of Witnesses is described in Chapter 12 – Witnesses.

❸ Sentences – control how the data entered in the Tag will appear in narrative reports. Use of Sentences is described in Chapter 11 – Working with Sentences.

❹ Sureties – provide a means to record the estimated reliability of the source. See page 54 for details.

❺ Name Variations – permit you to select married names, nicknames, etc., that you have entered in Name Tags. The selected name will be used for this event in narrative reports.

❻ Roles – can be assigned to show each person's part in the event and to enhance narrative reports by mentioning various participants in an event and their part in it. Use of Roles is described in Chapter 13 – Roles.

You switch between Beginner and Advanced modes in **Preferences > Program Options > Data Entry**. For a complete list of features enabled in Advanced mode, search Help for "Advanced."

Chapter 6 – Working with Sources

TMG has a comprehensive set of capabilities for recording source information that includes these features:

- Sources need be entered only once and then can be cited for any number of event, name, and relationship Tags.

- Citations link Sources to the Tags they support.

- Each Tag may have an unlimited number of Citations to different Sources.

- Reports produce footnotes or endnotes to document the recorded Citations.

- Bibliographies are available to list the Sources cited in reports.

- Footnotes or endnotes, and bibliographies, are automatically formatted based on popular style guides.

- Repositories need to be entered only once and then can be attached to any number of Sources.

This chapter is intended to help a new user better understand the basics of TMG's capabilities for managing sources and to offer some guidance for getting started in entering and citing Sources.

Understanding the Terms

Before we begin, it's helpful to have an understanding of the basic parts of the system.

A **_Source_** is something from which we have obtained information:

- It might be a book, letter, or e-mail. It could be a public record, tombstone, or census. It might also be an interview, or even our own memory.

- We describe a source by certain characteristics, such as title, author or creator, location, etc.

- In TMG, we describe each Source only once. That's called "creating a Source," or perhaps more properly, "creating a Source definition."

- Sources are listed in, and new Sources defined from, the Master Source List. The list is opened with the **Tools > Master Source List** menu command.

- Creating a Source definition doesn't associate that Source to any event we may record; that's done with a Citation, described next.

A **Citation** links the information recorded in a Tag to the Source of that information:

- When we enter a name, event, or relationship, we can add a Citation to show that information was found in a specific source.

- Citations are entered on the Citation screen, accessed from the Tag Entry Screen of the Tag that contains the information we obtained from the source.

- The Citation may also record details about how the source supports the information we entered. It may tell exactly where in the source the information was found, such as the page number. It may provide some detail about what the source said or how we interpreted it in recording what we entered in the Tag. For example, we might enter "shows age 16" when we enter a date in a Birth Tag, to record that the source had the age and that we computed the date from the age.

A **Repository** is a place where a source can be found:

- It might be a library where a book can be found, the archives where a public record is kept, or your own files where the letter from Aunt Jane is stored.

- Generally, style guides do not call for identifying Repositories for published works, such as books, since it is assumed that they can be found in many places. This information is usually called for with one-of-a-kind items, like deeds or private papers.

- Repositories are listed on, and new ones defined from, the Master Repository List, which is opened with the **Tools > Master Repository List** menu command.

- Repositories are attached to Source Definitions on the Attachments tab of the Source Definition screen.

- A Repository can be attached to any number of different Sources.

Source Types

Different types of sources are described differently, using characteristics appropriate for each type. The definition for a book, for example, might include title, author, and publisher, while one for a tombstone might include the name of the person and the name and address of the cemetery. When TMG produces footnotes or bibliography entries in reports, the items entered in the description appear in an order appropriate for the type of source, using italics, quotation marks, and other punctuation. TMG provides over 100 predefined **Source Types** to help create a Source definition that is appropriate for the particular kind of source you are defining. Source Types specify which characteristics of the source are to be recorded, and how the footnotes and bibliography entries will be formatted.

The default Source Types in the standard edition are based on Wholly Genes' interpretation of Elizabeth Shown Mills' *Evidence!* (*Evidence! Citation & Analysis for the Family Historian*, Baltimore: Genealogical Publishing Co., Inc., 1997). Those in the UK edition are based on designs by Caroline Gurney, specifically for sources commonly encountered in the United Kingdom.

With the general concepts now defined, how do we actually go about creating a Source definition? What follows is a step-by-step example of entering a new source and attaching it to a Tag. We are going to use a very common source as an example, an e-mail message from a relative.

Defining a Source

We open the Master Source List by using the **Tools > Master Source List** menu command. On that screen, click on the **Add** button to open the Source Types screen:

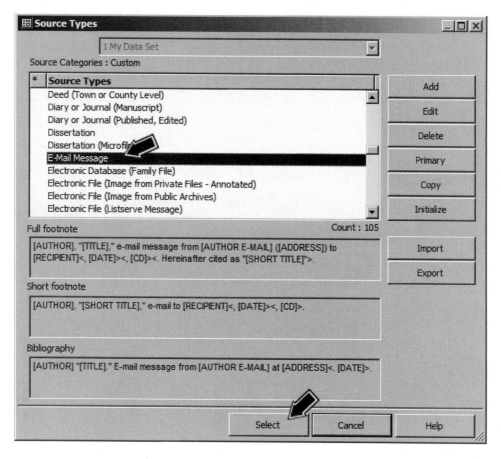

Since our example is an e-mail, we select the E-Mail Message Source Type and click **Select**. The **Select** button applies the E-mail Message source type we have selected and opens a Source Definition screen so we can create a Source of that type, as shown on the next page.

> Note: The **Add** button is a common source of confusion in this and similar screens. That button is for creating new Source Types, which would then be "Added" to this list. While we are in the process of adding a new Source, on this screen we are *selecting* a source type for our Source, so we use the **Select** button.

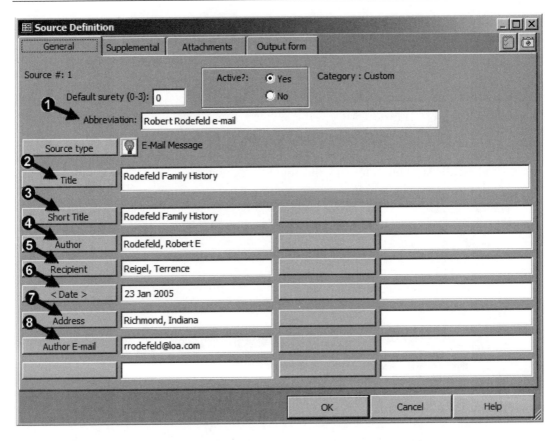

For this Source Type, we entered information into the following source elements:

❶ Abbreviation – always has to be filled in. It is used only on the Master Source List and on the Tag Entry and Citation screens to identify this Source. It is never included in any endnotes or bibliography, so enter any description that briefly describes this source to you.

❷ Title – is used for the "Subject" line of the e-mail in this Source Type. It could also be the title of a book or article. In some Source Types the label "title" appears in all lower case, which means it is not used and can be left empty. However, it is still a good idea to enter something for your own reference.

❸ Short Title – is used in footnotes after the first one for this source in a report. Repeat the Title if it's short, as in this case. If the Title is long enter a shortened version of it here.

❹ Author – is where we enter the name of the author (sender) of the e-mail. Generally enter names as shown, last name first, and TMG will rearrange the names properly for the full footnote, short footnote, and bibliography. If there is more than one name, separate them with semicolons, like this: Jones, Robert; Smith, Mary

❺ Recipient – is for the name of the person who received the e-mail, entered the same way.

❻ Date – is the date of the e-mail, in the format in which you want it to appear in notes. In this case, the label "<Date>" appears with angle brackets. That means that it may be omitted if desired without causing a problem in the footnotes. You might omit it if you choose to use this Source Definition for several different e-mails written on different days. If you did that you would enter the specific date in the Citation Detail when you cite this source (see next section).

❼ Address – is for the physical mailing address of the author. Entering a physical address in addition to the e-mail address is recommended because e-mail addresses change so often. Having a physical address offers a better chance of finding the author again later.

❽ Author E-mail – is for the e-mail address of the author.

> Note: If your Project was originally created in an earlier version of TMG, enter the address like this: \<rrodefeld@loa.com\>. The backslash characters causes the angle brackets, which have special meaning to TMG, to appear correctly in the output. Web addresses should be entered similarly in such Projects.

If you are unsure of what should be entered in any fields or the correct format to be used, consult the Reminder that should automatically appear if there is one for the Source Type. If it is set in **Preferences > Program Options > Data Entry** to not appear automatically, you can open it with the "light bulb" button next to the **Source Types** button. Some Source Types require the use of a Repository, as described on page 55, or an entry in the Comments field on the Supplemental tab. If so, the Reminder generally will mention that.

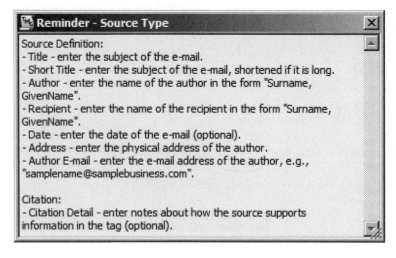

This e-mail example requires neither, so when all the fields on the General tab have been completed we click **OK** to close the Source Definition screen. We can see our newly created source listed in the Master Source List, as shown on the next page.

Note that the source is listed with its Abbreviation and the Source number, which is "1" in this case, because it is the first Source we have entered. Click **Close** to close the Master Source list. We have now completed the definition of our Source.

> Note: The **More >>** button at the lower right corner of the screen changes the Master Source List to a different display mode – if you see a **<< Less** button there, click it to return to this mode.

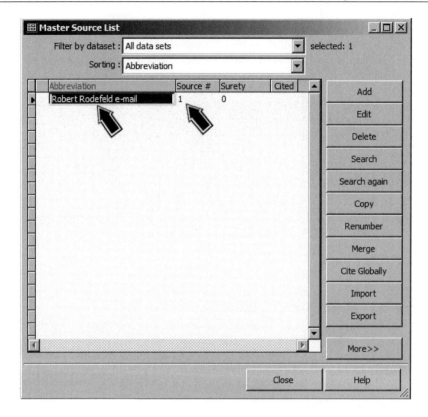

Testing Our Work

If we wanted to see the results of our work, we can go to the Output Forms tab of the Source Definition screen, as shown on the facing page.

Here we can see the three Source Templates that TMG uses to assemble the data we entered into completed footnotes or a bibliography. Next to each Template is a **Preview** button. Clicking those buttons opens a screen in which we can see a preview of how our notes will appear, as shown below.

The "<[CD]>" code appearing in the preview may be unexpected. It appears in the preview because the Citation Detail is not entered in the Source Definition, but is entered as part of each Citation when we cite this source. Since each Citation might have different information entered, the preview cannot know what that

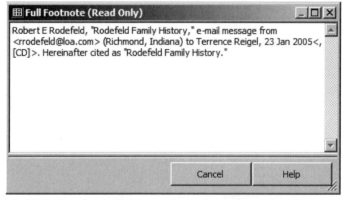

might be, so it simply displays the "<[CD]>" code to indicate where the information from the Citation Detail will appear in the actual note.

If something does not appear as we intended, we can go back to the General tab and modify our entries, or to the Supplemental tab or the Repository Definition screen if those are used by the Source Type we have selected. Or we may choose to edit the Source Template to adjust the output to our liking (see Chapter 15 – Customizing Sources).

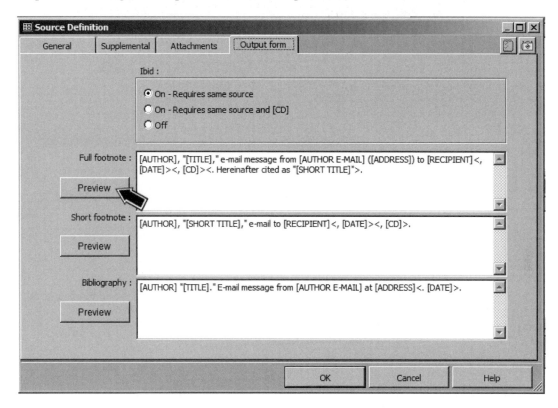

> Note: The Bibliography Template does not contain a "<[CD]>" code, and one might wonder why. The reason is that each Citation may have a different detail – and there is only one bibliography entry for the Source for the entire report. Since there would be no way to decide which Citation Detail to include, none is permitted.

Citing a Source

Now we are ready to "attach," or cite, this Source in an event Tag. We create a new Tag, or open an existing one, to cite our new Source. In the following example, we will use a Death Tag, because our correspondent provided information about the death of a cousin.

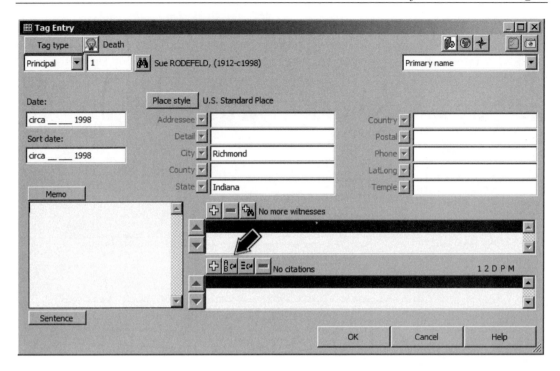

After the appropriate information is entered in the Date, Place, and/or Memo fields (see Chapter 5 – Entering and Editing Data), we are ready to add the Citation. We do that by clicking one of the three buttons near the bottom of the screen, above the (currently empty) list of citations:

Add New Citation – use this button if this is the first time you are citing this Source. It opens the Citation screen so you can enter the Source Number and other fields. You can use the F4 key instead of this button if you prefer.

Repeat Last Citation – use this button if you have previously cited this source and want to use the exact same Source and Citation Detail. This will add a Citation with the same Source number and Citation Detail used previously. It enters the Citation directly, without opening the Citation screen to allow entries in the other fields in that screen. You can use the F3 key instead of this button if you prefer.

Repeat Recent Citations – choose from a list of previously cited sources. The Citations screen then opens so you can edit the Citation Detail and enter data in the other fields if desired. You can use the Ctrl+F3 keys instead of this button if you prefer.

Using the Add New Citation or Repeat Recent Citations buttons opens the Citation screen, where you can complete the Citation, as shown on the facing page.

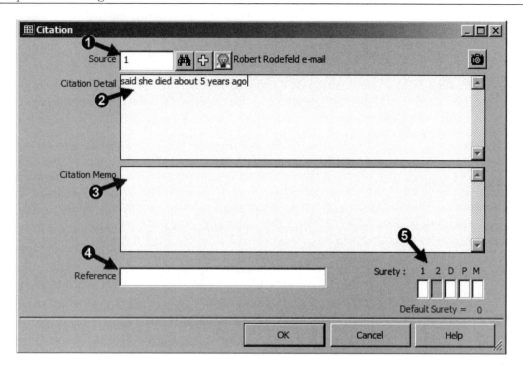

If we used the Add New Citation button, we enter data in the following fields in the Citation screen:

❶ **Source Number** – we can simply type the number in if we recall it. If not, click on the binoculars button next to the number field, which will open the Master Source List, and then select the desired source from that list. Note that when we move the cursor out of the source number field, the source Abbreviation appears to the right of the binoculars button, so we can be sure we have the right source.

❷ **Citation Detail** – here we enter any details we might want to record about this citation. In this case, our source, the e-mail, didn't give a date but said "she died about 5 years ago here in Richmond." But we entered a date – circa 1998 – in the Date field. So we explain that the source didn't actually give us the date, but we estimated it from the statement in the source. In other cases, like a book, we might enter a page number where the information appeared. If we had not entered the date of the e-mail in the source definition because we were using this source definition for several e-mails sent on different days, we might enter the date of the particular e-mail we used for this tag in the Citation Detail.

If we have used the Repeat Recent Citations button, the information from the previous Citation will be already entered, and we can edit it if we like.

If our Source had any special instructions for entering fields on the Citation screen, they should appear on the Reminder screen that opens when we select the Source. The Reminder is the same as described on page 49, unless a specific reminder has been created for this source.

There are three fields we are not using in this example:

❸ **Citation Memo** – is intended for transcription of the source text, or other notes about the source as it applies to this citation. It does not print in footnotes with the default Source Types but can be added by customizing the Source Templates (see Chapter 15 – Customizing Sources).

❹ **Reference** – is intended for entering a number from the user's personal file system. It does not print in footnotes with the default Source Types but can be added by customizing the Source Templates.

❺ **Surety** – is a shorthand way of indicating the expected reliability of the source in supporting the *data entered in this Tag* (not the reliability of the source overall). The five fields are to record the surety for the first and second Principal (that the source really refers to these people), and the Date, Place, and Memo (that the source is considered reliable in reporting the data entered in those fields). Allowed values are the numbers 0 through 3, with higher numbers being more reliable, and a minus sign, indicating that the source contradicts the data entered. Some users find using Sureties helpful, and others ignore them. Sureties are visible only if you are using the Advanced Data Entry mode.

TIP   Instead of using the repeat buttons above the Citation list, click the New Citation button, or press F4, to open the Citation screen. With that screen open, use the repeat keys described on page 41 to recall previously used entries for any of the fields.

When we are done, we click the **OK** button to return to the Tag Entry screen:

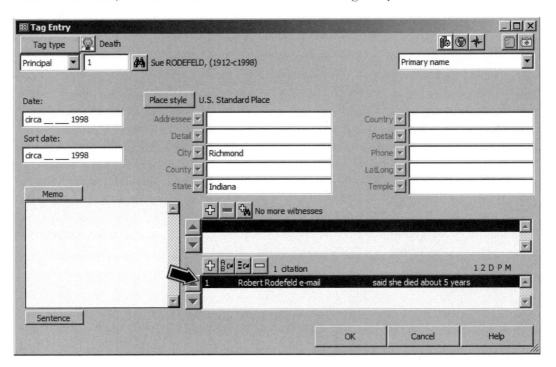

Note that the citation we just created is now shown in the list of Citations near the bottom of the screen. The listing includes the source Number, the source Abbreviation, and as much of the Citation Detail as will fit. If Surety values had been entered, they would appear after the fragment of the Citation Detail.

We're done! Click **OK** to exit the Tag Entry screen.

Repositories

Repositories are the places where a source can be found. TMG has a provision for recording Repositories separately and then attaching them to Sources as appropriate. This saves entering the same information repeatedly when you have several Sources from the same Repository. Because the e-mail Source used in the first example does not use a Repository, we will use as an example a Repository that might be created for a Birth Registration Source.

Use the **Tools > Master Repository List** menu command to open the Master Repository List. On that screen, we click the **Add** button to open the Repository Definition screen:

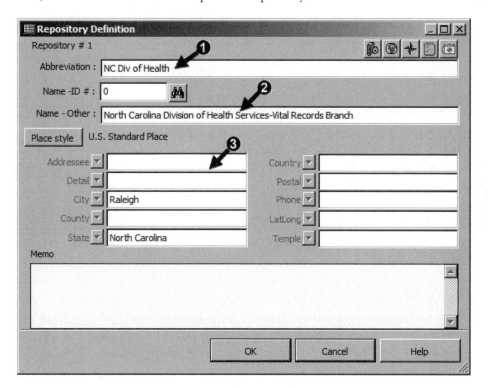

In this screen we have entered the data in the following fields:

❶ **Abbreviation** – a label that is used only to identify this Repository in the Master Repository List and in the Source Definition screen. The exact contents are not important so long as it is meaningful to us.

❷ **Name - Other** – the name of the Repository entered exactly as we want it to appear in the finished footnotes or bibliography listing.

❸ **Address fields** – the address of the repository, entering only the fields we want to appear in the notes.

When we have finished, we click the **OK** button and exit the Master Repository List. When we are ready to attach the Repository to a Source, we open the Source Definition screen for that Source, and click on the Attachments tab:

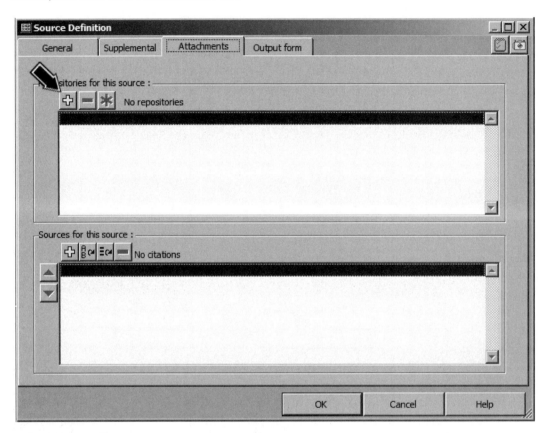

On that screen, we click the **+** button to open the Repository Link Entry screen:

On this screen we complete the following fields:

❶ Repository – type in the Repository number if we recall it, or click the binoculars (search) button to open the Master Repository List where we can select it.

❷ Reference – if there was a reference number, like a manuscript number at an archive, we would enter that number in this field.

Click **OK** to return to the Source Definition screen, where we now see our Repository attached to the Source:

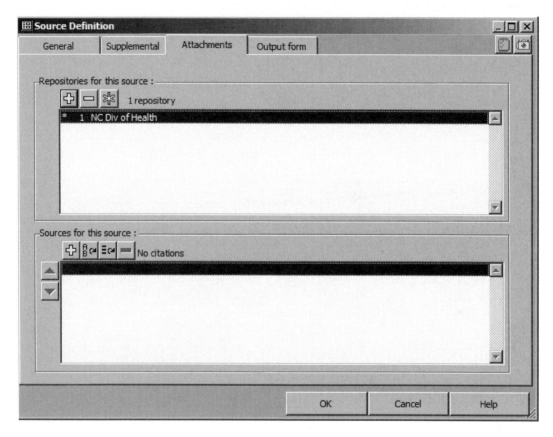

We can attach more than one Repository to any Source, but only the one marked Primary (with the asterisk in front of it) will be used in the printed notes.

Chapter 7 – Setting Up Reports

The Master Genealogist offers a wide variety of reports, which can be conveniently divided into two groups. One group is primarily designed to aid in research tasks. Most of these produce lists of people, events, etc., that meet a specified set of criteria. This group is described in Chapter 8 – Reports for Research and Analysis. The second group is primarily designed to communicate our findings to others, and to record them for posterity. They include various charts, forms, and narrative reports and are described in Chapter 9 – Genealogy Reports.

Each report is controlled by a Report Definition screen, which defines who or what the subjects of the report are to be and whether the report is to be displayed on screen, printed, or made into a file for another program. The actual generation of the report is also controlled from this screen. This chapter describes the use of that screen to set up and generate reports.

The Report Definition Screen

All reports are started from the Report menu by selecting the desired report, which opens the Report Definition screen for that report. The screenshot below shows the one for the List of People report, which is identical to those for most of the reports described in Chapter 9 – Genealogy Reports. Those for the other types of reports are generally similar.

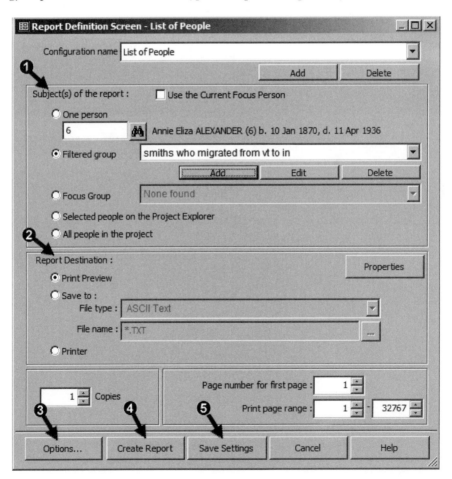

The most commonly used features of the Report Definition screen are described below:

❶ **Subjects Box** – specifies the *Subjects* of the report – that is, which people, events, citations, or whatever are to be included in the report.

❷ **Report Destination** – controls where the finished report is to be sent. It can be sent to your computer screen as a preview and then printed if desired, created as a file to be opened in a word processor or other application, or be sent directly to your printer.

❸ **Options Button** – opens the report Options screen, the contents of which vary depending on the specific report being used. Those options are discussed in the next two chapters.

❹ **Create Report Button** – causes the report to be generated. If you have changed any of the settings on the Report Definition screen or in Options, those changes are saved for use if you want to generate the report again.

❺ **Save Settings Button** – saves the settings you have made in the Report Definition. Use this button when you have changed some settings and then decide you don't want to make the report just yet but do want to save the changes you have made.

Specifying the Subject Elements of the Report

Each Report Definition has a Subjects section in which you specify which people, citations, events, or the like are to be included in the report. The methods available depend on the type of report being used. Those for the List of People report are shown in the screenshot on the previous page, and are the most extensive of any report:

- **One Person** – requires you to either enter the person's ID number or check the "Use the Current Focus Person" box to have the definition change to the current focus person each time you open the report definition. This option is primarily used for the reports described in Chapter 9 – Genealogy Reports.

- **Filtered Group** – is probably the most useful way of specifying the subjects of the reports covered in Chapter 8 – Reports for Research and Analysis, and is occasionally useful for the others as well. Each report has a set of filters specific to the type of data that report produces. There are hundreds of thousands of possible combinations available, allowing users to create a virtually endless number of customized reports. Creation of Filters is discussed later in this chapter.

- **Focus Group** – is an easy way to specify a group of people that may be difficult to specify with a Filter. Use of the Focus Group is described on page 22. To use this method, create the Focus Group before opening the Report Definition. You can also save Focus Groups and use a saved group, rather than the current one, to control the subjects of the report. This method only applies to reports whose subjects are people or names.

- **Selected People in the Project Explorer** – is an alternate way to specify a group of people. The Project Explorer is discussed on page 21. To use this method, open the Project Explorer before opening the Report Definition. In the Project Explorer, select the desired people. Use standard Windows techniques to select a group of people – select the first and then hold the Shift key while clicking on the last to select a continuous group, or hold Ctrl while clicking on individuals to select a discontinuous group. This method only applies to reports whose subjects are people or names.

- **All People** – is generally only useful for small Projects because of the large number of subjects that will be included.

Output to Screen, Printer, or File

You specify where TMG is to send your report in the "Report Destination" box that occupies most of the lower half of the Report Definition screen. If you select "Print Preview," the report will appear on your computer screen, where you can view it, and if you like, then send it to your printer. If you select "Printer" the report is sent directly to your printer.

Often the most useful option is "Save To" – meaning that a computer file is created that can then be opened in another application. The available formats vary by the type of report, but generally include the following:

- Adobe® Acrobat® format ("PDF"), which can be read with Adobe Reader® software and other programs.

- Several varieties of text files, which can be read with many applications.

- Many word processor formats, including those of Microsoft Word and Corel® WordPerfect® programs.

- Several spreadsheet formats, available only in the "List of…" reports.

To create a report as a file, you select the Save To option and then select the desired File Type from the drop-down list. Enter a file name in the File Name field. If you have not used this option before, the default name will be something like " *.pdf " or " *.doc " – change the " * " to the name you want to use for the file.

Click the **Create Report** button to create the report. When it is completed TMG will offer to open it in the application registered on your computer for that file type. You can also open the report file later with that application. The default file location will be in a folder called Report_output, which is a subfolder of the "The Master Genealogist v7" folder, which itself is a subfolder of your normal document location, such as "My Documents." You can change that default location when you assign the file name in the Report Definition screen, or change it for all new reports in **Preferences > Current Program Options > Advanced**.

Once you have opened the report file in its normal program, you can edit it, print it, or do anything else you might do with a document created with that application.

Using Filters

The *Filters* in TMG's reports allow you to create an almost unlimited number of custom reports. A Filter allows you to specify which people, citations, events, etc., are to be included in the report based on one or more criteria. Thus, a List of People report might be limited to people born in Virginia, a List of Citations report might contain only Citations to Source number 123, or a List of Events report might include only events in the city of New York.

Each type of report has its own set of filter elements specific to the subject of that report, but each works in a similar way. In the remainder of this chapter we will examine the Filters for people, because they are probably the most commonly used type. People Filters are used not only in the List of People report, but also in the reports discussed in Chapter 9 – Genealogy Reports. They can also be used to filter the Picklist and Project Explorer.

The filters of the other reports are similar in concept, so the principles illustrated here should help with those filters as well.

TMG comes with several example people Filters:

- Females who are not living
- People whose given name begins with john
- People who are adopted
- People with more than six children
- Women whose given name contains liz

To try these Filters open the Report Filter screen for the List of People report. Select Filtered Group in the Subjects box and select one of the sample Filters from the drop-down list. You could run a report with the selected filter, or click the **Edit** button to examine how the Filter is constructed.

Query by Example Filters

The people Filters have a special mode of operation, called "Query by Example," intended to simplify the creation of basic Filters. We will consider that mode first because it provides a useful introduction to several filter principles.

Filters are specified on the Report Filter screen. Open that screen from the Report Definition screen by selecting Filtered Group and clicking the **Add** button below the Filter drop-down window. Click on the Query by Example tab on the Report Filter screen to see a screen like that in the screenshot on the next page.

In this screenshot we have created a filter designed to find only those people with surname of Smith who migrated from Vermont to Indiana.

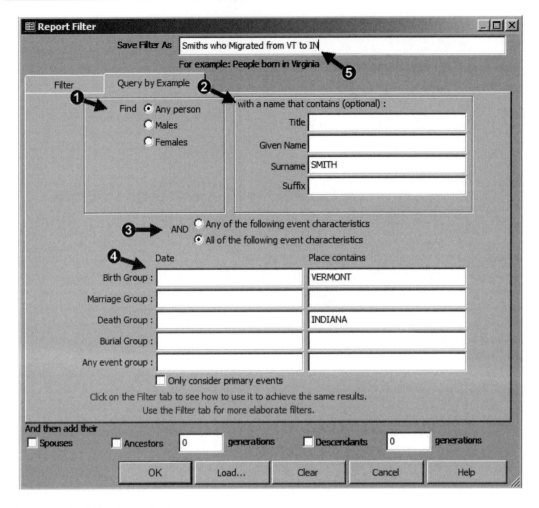

We made the following selections:

❶ **Find box** – selected "Any Person" because we wanted both males and females.

❷ **Name box** – entered only a surname. We could have also entered a given name, or a title or suffix, but we wanted all Smith relatives.

❸ **AND choice** – selected "All of the following event characteristics" because we want only those who both were born in Vermont and who died in Indiana. (Selecting the "Any of the following event characteristics" option would give us everyone born in Vermont *and* everyone who died in Indiana.)

❹ **Event list** – entered for the Birth Group that the place contains "Vermont" and for the Death Group that the place contains "Indiana." We could have entered any combination of dates and places, but no more were needed for our example.

❺ **Filter Name** – entered a name for this Filter so we can find it if we want to use it again in the future. If you don't expect to use the Filter again, leaving the default name is fine.

When we have finished specifying the Filter, we click **OK** to return to the Report Definition screen, where we can proceed to create the report.

Creating a Filter Line-by-Line

The Query by Example method is easier to use than specifying a filter line-by-line, but is limited in its flexibility. To understand the more capable method of specifying the filter directly, click on the Filter tab to see the filter created by our Query by Example exercise:

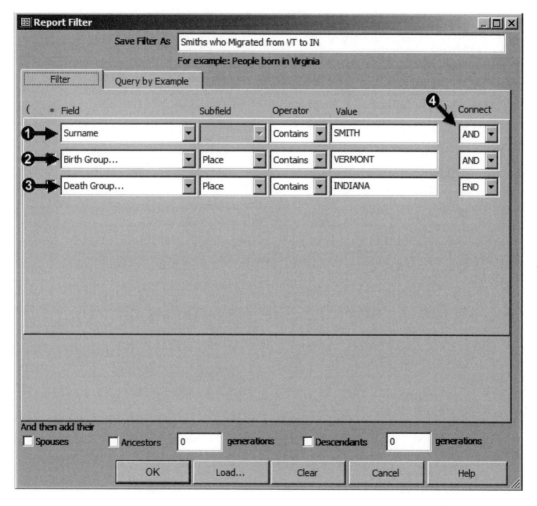

Here we see that the specifications we entered in the Query by Example mode have been converted into three lines, each with several elements. The lines correspond to the information we entered in the Query by Example mode:

● There is no line for sex because we specified "all people." Had we specified either males or females, there would be a line for that term.

❶ Our specification to use the surname Smith appears as a line that says that the Surname of the person must contain "SMITH."

❷ Our specification that a Birth Group Tag is to include the state of Vermont appears as a line that says a Birth Group Tag must have a place that includes "VERMONT."

❸ Our specification that a Death Group Tag is to include the state of Indiana appears as a line that says a Death Group Tag must have a place that includes "INDIANA."

❹ The lines are "connected" with AND because we specified that we wanted people who have surname Smith and are both born in Vermont and died in Indiana.

The "connector" function seems to cause a lot of confusion among users. The choices are AND or OR. The technical term for this is Boolean Logic, but to many users it seems contrary to ordinary logic. It may help to think of this in the following terms:

- We want people who were born in Vermont AND who died in Indiana. Both conditions must apply.

- We do not want people who were born in Vermont OR who died in Indiana. That would include those who were born in Vermont and never stepped foot in Indiana, as well as those who died in Indiana and never laid eyes on Vermont.

If we had created the filter directly, instead of using the Query by Example method, we would have used the drop-down lists to select the Fields – Surname, Birth Group… and Death Group… in this example. Some Fields have Subfields, such as the Birth Group… and Death Group… fields in this example. If so, select the Subfield from its drop-down list.

Next we would select the Operator. The Query by Example method generally uses the Operator "Contains." If we created the filter directly we would have had a choice of many others, including Equals, Begins with, Does not contain, and Is empty. The available Operators differ depending on the Field and Subfield selected.

In most cases, the desired text in the Value field is simply typed in, although in a few cases there is a drop-down list. The Connect value is selected from its drop-down list. Selecting AND or OR opens the next line for an additional term.

Filters other than "people" Filters can only be created line-by-line. The main reason to use the line-by-line method of creating a people Filter is to create a more complex Filter than can be created with the Query by Example method. For example, suppose in the Filter we constructed above we wanted to include people who had moved to Indiana but did not die there (or we have no record of their death). We could do that by adding a new line, entered on the Filter tab, as shown in the screenshot on the facing page.

We now want to include people who died in Indiana OR those who had any other event recorded there, like a census, occupation, etc.

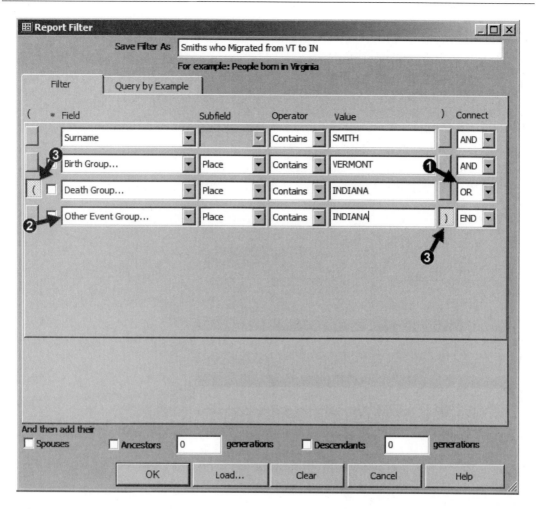

We have made the following changes to the filter we previously defined:

❶ We change the END Connector on the last line to an OR Connector. When we change END to AND or OR, a new line appears so we can add another term to the Filter.

❷ We create the new term, starting by selecting "Other Event Group…" from the Field drop-down list. We select "Place" from the Subfield drop-down list. We select "Contains" from the Operator drop-down list. Then we type in "INDIANA" in the Value field.

❸ When we choose the OR Connector, boxes appear on either side of each line. If we click on them, parentheses display and can be used to group the terms. In this case, we want people who were born in Vermont AND also either {died in Indiana OR had another event there}. We click on two of those boxes to reveal the parentheses, grouping the items just as they are in the preceding sentence.

Adding Spouses, Ancestors, and Descendants

There is a useful function at the bottom of the People Filter screen that allows us to add the spouses, ancestors, or descendants of the people specified in the body of the Filter. (This feature is only available when using the filter for reports, not when using it in the Picklist and Project Explorer.) This is often a convenient way to add others one wants to include, but it is easy to misunderstand how the feature works and get unexpected results. Suppose we create this filter:

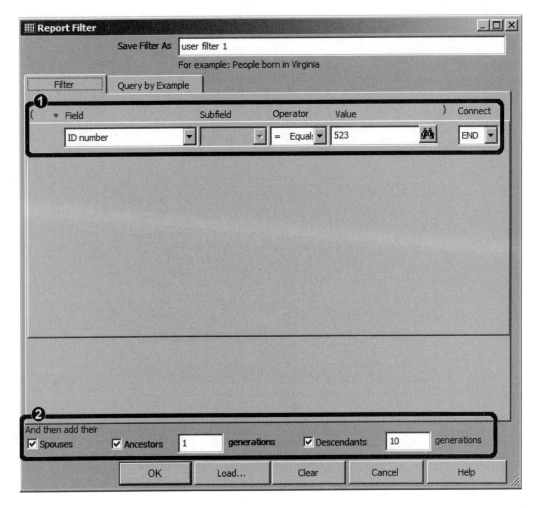

We have specified that the Filter is to include the person whose ID number is 523, as can be seen in the outlined area near the top of the screen. Then in the outlined area near the bottom of the screen, we said "And then add their…" Spouses, Ancestors for one generation, and Descendants for ten generations. In other words, we are asking for

❶ The person whose ID number is 523, in the upper area of the screen.

❷ Then, in the lower part of the screen we add

- The Spouses of the person whose ID number is 523.

- The Ancestors for one generation, that is, the parents, of the person whose ID number is 523.

- The Descendants for ten generations of the person whose ID number is 523.

The common error is to expect we will also get the spouses of the Descendants. But that is not what we asked for. The Spouses, Ancestors, and Descendants terms at the bottom of the screen each refer independently to the person or persons defined by the main body of the Filter. They do not refer to each other, so the Spouses term does not apply to those added by the Ancestors or Descendants terms.

TIP

In the examples above we have typed text into the Value field to create our Filters, such as the ID number in the last example. If we then wanted a similar Filter for a different ID number, we have to edit the Filter to change the Value. A useful alternative is to enter the code [?] in place of the Value. When we do that, TMG asks us to supply the value each time the report is run, making it easy to use the same filter with different values each time. See page 70 for an example of using this technique.

Chapter 8 – Reports for Research and Analysis

The reports described in this chapter are primarily designed as aids in research tasks. Most of them produce lists of people, events, etc., that meet a specified set of criteria. For example, before undertaking a search of death records in a specific state, you might create a list of all people who lived in that state. Most of the reports in this group are found on the **Reports > List of...** menu. In this chapter we discuss the three of them that are most commonly used:

<u>Report</u>	<u>Typical Applications</u>
List of People	Listing selected people for a research project.
	Setting a Flag for a particular list of people.
List of Events	Finding all events in a specific place.
List of Citations	Finding all citations to a specific Source.

The set-up of these reports, including the specification of who or what is to be included, and where the finished report is to be delivered, is described in Chapter 7 – Setting Up Reports. In this chapter we discuss the considerations specific to this group of reports.

We discuss below each of the three reports, followed by some features common to most of the reports in the group. Because all the List of… reports work in a similar way, understanding this foundation should enable effective use of the others. The remaining List of… reports are

- List of Names
- List of Tag Types
- List of Places
- List of Tasks
- List of Repositories
- List of Witnesses
- List of Sources

The chapter concludes with a brief description of some unique analysis reports.

The List of People Report

The List of People report has two distinct primary uses – creating research lists and managing process tasks on groups of people.

The more common one is just what the name implies, to create a list of people for some research task. A few examples of this use are

- You are going to visit a local historical society and want a list of all the people known to have lived in the area. You might create a list of everyone for whom you have recorded an event in that place.

- You are planning to search Civil War records and want a list of all the men who might have served in that war. You might create a list of everyone whose birth dates suggest they would have been at the appropriate age, and who had not died before the war.

- You have found that a state where your relatives lived has images of death records available online and want a list of those people whose records might be found. You might create a list of all those who died in that state during the period of the available records. If your Project does not include a death record for some of the people, you might create a list of anyone with any event in that state.

The key to creating all these lists is to define the group of people you have in mind. In the examples above, the group would be defined with Filters (discussed starting on page 61). Other lists might consist of a set of related people, say all the ancestors of a person, the children of those ancestors, and the spouses of those children. For these lists, a Focus Group may be easier to set up (use of the Focus Group is described on page 22).

In most cases you will want to check the settings in Options for the Output Columns to make sure the resulting list will include the information needed for your research (see the section starting on page 71). There are other settings available in Options, such as the fonts to be used, but generally they are unimportant in a working document such as this.

If your list is to be used only while editing data in TMG or while doing online research, you may just send it to your screen. If you want to check off names as you review them, or take a copy on a research trip, a printed copy may be best. Or you may want to send the report to a word processor or to a spreadsheet program for further editing or analysis.

A less common, but very valuable, use of the List of People report is to execute a processing task on a group of people in your Project. For example you might wish to change Flag settings for a specific group, or you might wish to create a new Project containing selected people to send to another researcher. In these cases you would use the Secondary Output, as described beginning on page 72.

The List of Events Report

The List of Events report generates lists of event Tags that meet specific criteria. It lists only Event Tags – those for Birth, Marriage, Death, Census, etc. It will not include Name Tags (use the List of Names for that) nor will it include parent/child Relationship Tags.

For this report, the subject events are almost always defined with a Filter. There is probably no single dominant use for this report, but the large number of filter combinations possible makes it a very versatile report for identifying events meeting a large number of criteria. For example, this Filter

Field	Subfield	Operator	Value	Connect
Number of Citations		> Is greater than	9	END

will find all events with more than nine citations.

This filter

Field	Subfield	Operator	Value	Connect
Memo		Contains	ROUND LAKE	END

will find all events in which the term "Round Lake" is entered in the Memo.

This filter

Field	Subfield	Operator	Value	Connect
Tag Type...	Label	= Equals	CENSUS	AND
Number of Other Witness		> Is greater than	1	END

will find all census tags that have more than one person attached as a Witness.

A creative user can find many more applications for this versatile report.

The List of Citations Report

The List of Citations report is generally a "working" report used to find information about the citations entered in your data base. Perhaps the most common use is to locate all the citations to a specific Source. That can be done with the following filter:

Field	Subfield	Operator	Value	Connect
Source Number		= Equals	[?]	END

You could enter the source number directly in the Value field, but then if you wanted to search for a different Source you would have to open the Filter and edit it. By entering the code [?] in the value field you are asked each time you run the report which Source to use.

Another application of the List of Citations report is to find a bit of text you have entered in the Citation Detail of a Citation, but you can't recall for which person. For that application, you might use a filter like the following:

Field	Subfield	Operator	Value	Connect
Citation Detail		Contains	[?]	END

When you run the report, type in the bit of text you are searching for when prompted.

The List of Citations report can use the columnar output arrangement used by most of the other "List of..." reports. But by default it uses an "Indented" output format, which groups the citations by source, and within each source lists the Tag Type, Date if the Tag is dated, the Principal or Principals with their ID numbers, and the Place. You specify which output form is to be used in the "List Type" box on the General tab of report Options.

TIP

With the "Indented" output format, there is an option on the General tab of Options to "Include sureties." Using this option causes the listed citations to be sorted by the sureties assigned in the Citation, which is generally not helpful. I recommend un-checking this option unless you specifically need it.

Specifying the Output

Many of the reports in this group produce their output in columns. The contents and layout of those columns can be specified by the user. The specific contents available vary by the report type but typically include names of people, their ID numbers, dates and places of various Tags, and many special items peculiar to the subject of a specific report.

The output columns are specified on the Output Columns tab of the Report Options screen, which is opened by clicking the **Options** button at the lower left corner of the Report Definition screen. Here is that screen for the List of People report:

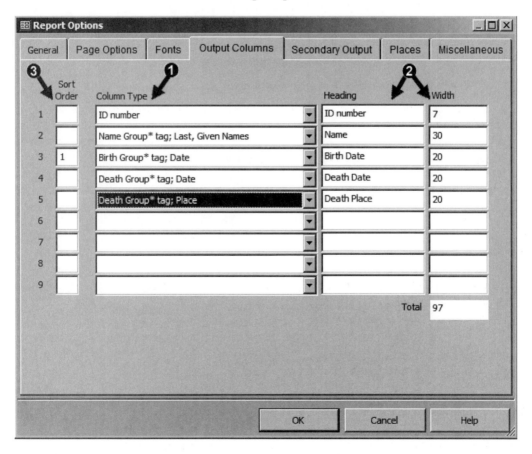

Each row on the screen corresponds to a column in the finished report. We specify what is to be in each column of the report as described on the following page.

❶ We select the desired contents from the drop-down list in the Column Type column. Here we have selected the subject's ID number for the first column, then the person's name in Surname, Given Name format, followed by Birth date, Death date, and Death Place. These are but a few of the approximately 300 options available for this report. The other List of... reports offer choices appropriate for their subjects.

❷ For each Column Type there is a default column Heading and column Width, which are automatically entered in those fields when the Column Type is selected. They are generally satisfactory, but you can edit either if you like.

❸ The output is sorted based on the numbers entered in the Sort Order column. Here we have entered a 1 in the Birth Date column, so the results will be sorted by that date. If we wanted we could enter a 2, 3, etc., in other lines to create further sorts on those items.

Some of the reports in the analysis group do not use the multi-column output format, or offer it as an alternative to a different format. For example, the List of Sources report offers a choice among listing of Abbreviations, Titles, or Bibliographic form, or the multi-column format; the List of Repositories report offers only a choice between a list of the Abbreviation or Name of the Repository. These choices are specified on the General tab of Options

Secondary Output

One of the more useful but often overlooked features of the List of People and List of Events reports is the ability to change Flag settings for the people listed in the report, create new Projects or Data Sets containing those people, and make other changes in your Project.

To use this feature, first define a list of people or events using one of the methods to specify the Subject(s) of the report on the Report definition screen. Then, in report Options, use the Secondary Output tab to specify which change you want to make for the people listed in the report.

The key is to define the group of people or events on which you want the Secondary Output to act. Using a Filter is often the best method, but for the List of People report, sometimes a Focus Group may be easier to set up.

Once you have defined the group of people or events the Secondary Output is to act on, you specify what that action will be on the Secondary Output tab of the Report Definition screen, as shown in the screenshot on the facing page.

Once you have set the options and specified the subjects of the report, use the **Create Report** button on the Report Definition screen to create the report. After the report is created (or immediately, if you checked the "Suppress output" option), you will be asked to confirm that the action specified on the Secondary Output tab is to be completed. Click **Yes** to compete the action or **No** if for some reason you decide not to complete it.

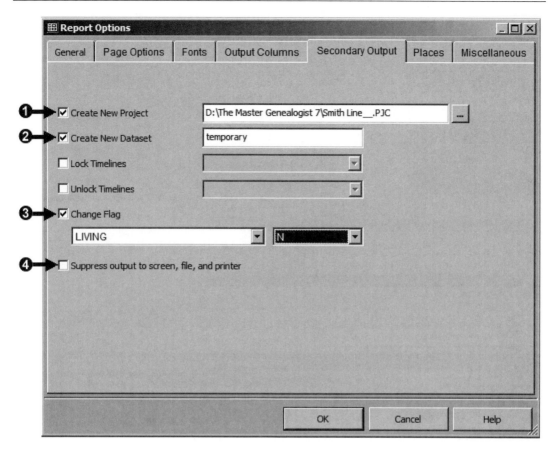

This is the Secondary Output tab for the List of People report. The most useful options are

❶ **Create a new Project** – copying from the current Project only those people who are on the List of People. When this option is checked, you enter the name and location of the new Project in the field provided.

❷ **Create a new Data Set** – within the current Project, copying from the current Data Set only those people who are on the List of People. When this option is checked, you enter the name of the new Data Set in the field provided.

❸ **Change a selected Flag** – to a specific value for those people who are on the List of People. When this option is checked, you select the flag you want to change from the drop-down list then select the value you want the flag changed to from the second drop-down list. In the example, we are having the Living Flag set to N.

> Note: In the screenshot all three of these options are checked for illustration. In practice, one would usually check only one of them.

❹ **Suppress output** – to screen, file, or printer. If you are sure the list you have defined includes the correct people, you can save time by checking this option so that the actual report is not displayed but is used only to produce the specified Secondary Output.

The Secondary Output of the List of Events report has only the option for changing Flags. Since Flags are associated with people and that report deals with events, you have to specify which people attached to the Tags are to have their Flag changed. Choices are first, second, or both Principals; Other Witnesses; All Witnesses (includes Principals); or people with a specific Role.

Other Analysis Reports

In addition to the List of ... reports, there are several other reports in the analysis group. We will simply mention them and suggest your explore them on your own:

- **Audit** – examines your data for apparent errors, such as parents of improbable ages, events before birth or after death, etc. The items to be evaluated are controlled on the Miscellaneous tab of Options for that report.

- **Distribution of People** – provides the frequency of occurrence of specific names.

- **Project Information** – lists the number of people, names, events, etc., in the Project.

- **Statistical Report** – provides various statistics about the people in your Project, such as the average age at marriage, age at death, etc.

Chapter 9 – Genealogy Reports

In this chapter we discuss those reports intended primarily for sharing your data with others. These reports include

- The traditional genealogy forms – Family Group Sheets, Pedigree Charts and others.

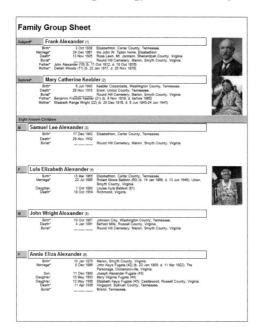
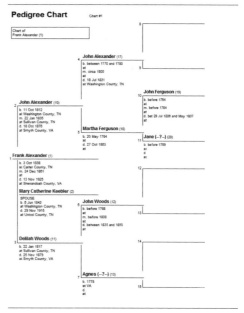

- Narrative reports in various styles, including Journal style and Ahnentafels, all in true narrative style with full sentence text.

- Box style tree charts in several configurations, with the ability to edit the finished charts to achieve customized results.

Descendant Box Chart

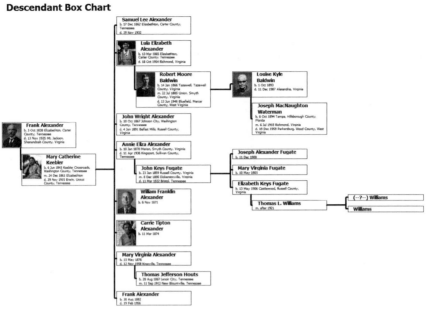

The "thumbnail" views above provide only a general idea of the various types of reports. A good way to get a better understanding of all the report types is to look at the sample reports posted on the Wholly Genes website. You can view them with **the Report > Sample Reports web site** menu command in TMG. There are several examples of each type of report showing the results of various optional settings.

Another way to become familiar with the available reports is to create a sample using the default settings. Then print a copy of any that might be of interest, label them, and keep them in a folder for future reference.

The setup of these reports, including specifying who or what is to be included and in which form the finished report is to be delivered, is described in Chapter 7 – Setting Up Reports. In this chapter we discuss the various considerations and options specific to this group of reports. We will start with those features shared by most or all of the reports in this group then move on to the specific aspects of each type.

Selecting the Subjects of the Report

The general discussion of specifying the subjects of reports on page 59 applies, with one very important distinction. Only two reports in this group, the Individual Narrative and the Individual Detail reports, are about a single person. For those two reports, you can specify one person or a group of people as subjects. If you specify a group you will get a set of reports, with one report for each person.

All the other reports and charts in the group are ancestor or descendant reports. That is, they have a starting person, and then show the ancestors or descendants of that person. For these reports you *specify only the starting person* as the subject. The report itself, guided by the options you specify, determines who else is to be included.

TIP

Rather than set the subject of ancestor and descendant reports manually each time you create a report, leave the "Use the Current Focus Person" option at the top of the Report Definition screen checked. Then navigate to the desired starting person before opening the Report Definition. The starting person is automatically selected for you when you open that screen.

On rare occasions you may want to specify a number of starting persons as subjects for these reports. When you do that TMG produces a set of ancestor or descendant reports, with each report in the set starting with one of the people you specified. For most types of reports, if the trees in the individual reports in the set overlap, a cross-reference is provided and the duplicates are omitted.

Controlling Who is Included

Most ancestor and descendant reports and charts will include a specified number of generations of ancestors and descendants. You set that number on the General tab of Options for each report.

Several of the reports offer additional options to control who is included. In the Ancestor Box Chart you can include siblings of the ancestors. You can include spouses in the Descendant Indented Chart and the descendants Journal report. The Descendant Indented Narrative can be set to include only those with the starting person's surname. All of these options are found on the Miscellaneous or Other tab of report Options.

Sources, Endnotes, and Bibliographies

Excepting the Box Charts, most of the reports and charts in this group provide for source citations to be included. The same reports and charts have provision for creating a bibliography of the sources cited.

Sources are enabled from the Sources tab of Options for each report, as shown on the screenshot on the next page. The most commonly used options are described below the screenshot.

Bibliographies are enabled from the Publication Tools tab of Options for each report. A bibliography can be created only if Sources are also enabled in the report.

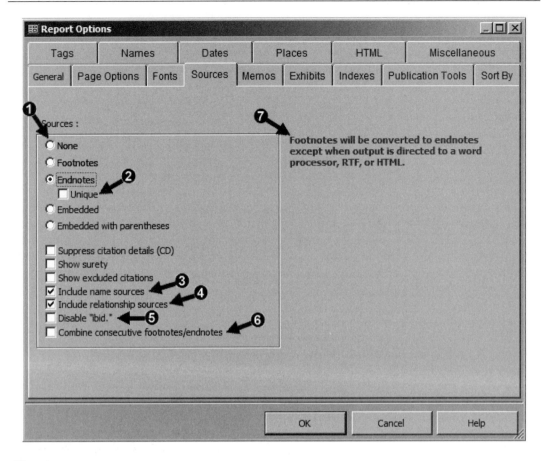

❶ **Enabling Sources** – you enable Source notes by choosing to use Footnotes or Endnotes. In narrative reports, you can also choose to have them embedded in the text.

Once Sources are enabled, a number of useful options are available:

❷ **Unique Endnotes** – are available if you choose Endnotes. With *Unique Endnotes*, if an endnote would be exactly the same as any previous endnote, it is not repeated, and the reference number refers to the previous instance of that note.

❸ **Name Sources** – may be included. If they are, their reference numbers for the Primary Name Tag appear immediately after the first mention of the person's name.

❹ **Relationship Sources** – may be included as well. If they are, their reference numbers appear immediately after those for the Primary Name. Since they cannot readily be distinguished from those for the Name, and often refer to the same Sources, many users find this option produces confusing results.

❺ **Ibid.** – replaces a note with "Ibid." when it refers to the same Source as the previous footnote. Ibid., short for the Latin *Ibidem*, meaning "the same place," was once common in formal works but is used less now. There are also controls on the Output Forms tab of the Source Definition screen that control how Ibid. will be used for a given Source, if at all.

❻ **Combine Consecutive Notes** – combines several citations in a single Tag into a single footnote, eliminating the string of note reference numbers that would otherwise occur.

❼ **Endnote Notice** – is a reminder that footnotes will become endnotes unless the report is being created as a word processor, rich text, or HTML file.

The procedure for actually creating the source notes and bibliography differs depending on where the finished report is sent:

- **Word Processor or RTF File** – if you have the report created as a word processor or rich text file (RTF), the footnotes or endnotes will be included in the file. They will generally be encoded using the word processor's footnote or endnote format, which means that all the automatic functions the word processor has for processing footnotes and endnotes will be available if you edit the file in the word processor. For example, if you delete a note, the remaining notes will be renumbered. (Exception: If you use the Unique Endnotes option, the notes are produced as plain text, and the word processor's note features do not apply.)

  TIP
  If you create a report containing footnotes or endnotes as a word processor file, and do not see them in the word processor the problem is usually the view setting in the word processor. Change the view to Page Layout, Print Layout, or similar to have the notes display.

  If bibliographies are specified they will also be included in the file.

- **Screen, Printer, or PDF File** – if you send the report to screen, directly to your printer, or have it created as a PDF or text file, the note reference numbers are added to the text, but the notes themselves are not included. Instead, they are accumulated so that you can create a single set of notes for several reports in a set if you like. When you are ready to print the endnotes, you do that with the Endnotes report. Print the bibliography with the Bibliography report.

Controlling Formatting

There are a wide variety of controls on the various report Options tabs to control the formatting of the data elements that appear in reports, as well as the page layout itself. For example, options on the Names tab allow names to appear in mixed case or upper case and control the display of identifiers, such as the ID number. The Date and Places tabs allow control of formatting of those elements. The Page Options and Fonts tabs allow control of the page itself. Most of the reports have a Miscellaneous tab which controls options specific to that report type.

The best way to learn about the available options is to scan each of the tabs on the Options screen. If the meaning of any is unclear, click the **Help** button, which leads to a description of each item on the screen.

Specifying Report Content

The **Ahnentafel**, **Journal**, **Family Group Sheet**, **Narrative**, and **Individual Detail** reports all provide extensive control of the Tags that are to be included in the report. Those controls appear on the Tags tab of report Options, as shown below.

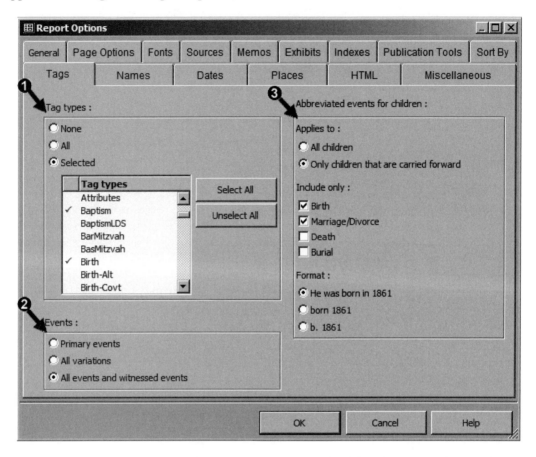

This screenshot is of the Options for the Journal Report, which has three sets of controls:

❶ **Tag Types** – controls which Tag Types are included. You can specify that none or all are included, or you can select specific types you want to appear. When you choose the Selected option, the list of Tag Types appears, and any number of Tag Types may be selected. Each type is selected or unselected by double-clicking on it. Here the Baptism and Birth Tag Types have been selected, as indicated by the check marks.

The Selected option is useful in creating a "bare-bones" report in which you want to include only a few Tag Types. It is also a handy way to exclude various notes that you might not want to print, provided you have entered them in a unique Tag Type – simply unselect that Tag Type.

❷ **Events** – allows you to specify "Primary events," "All variations," or "All events and witnessed events."

❸ **Other Controls** – are available for some reports. In the Journal report, shown here, you can further control which events are included in the lists of children that follow each person's narrative. The Family Group Sheet has options that will further control which events will appear for the subject, spouse, and children.

The **Compressed Pedigree** and **Descendant Indented** charts simply allow you to select among the primary Birth, Marriage, Death, and Burial Tags on the Tags tab.

The **Box Charts** use a totally different method of specifying which tags are used. On the Data Types tab of report Options, you can specify which Tag data is to appear on up to nine lines in each box, with separate specifications for various people depending on how they are related to the focus person.

All the reports and charts, except the Box charts, have an option to **Suppress details for living persons**. That option is found on the Miscellaneous tab of report Options. If it is selected, for everyone whose Living Flag is set to "Y" or "?" only names and a message like "is still living" will appear.

The **Surety** setting is found on the General tab of Options for most reports. It is intended to allow exclusion of data that is of questionable reliability, based on the Surety values entered in Citations (see page 54). Using it for that purpose requires consistent entry of Sureties in your Project.

TIP

This option is often the source of unexpected results. If the value set for the report is higher than the highest Surety entered in a Tag, the information in that Tag is omitted from the report. Accidentally setting this option too high can result in data, or even whole people, being omitted from the report. If you do not intend to restrict any content the *safest setting is "No Threshold," with "Include blank surety"* checked as well. This is illustrated as item 4 on the screenshot on the next page.

Narrative Reports

TMG's narrative style reports produce true narrative text – all the output is in complete sentences, as one would create if writing a narrative manually. The narrative output is controlled by the Sentence Structure in each Tag, as discussed in Chapter 11 – Working with Sentences. Using default Sentences, the text may seem somewhat repetitive, reading like the computer-generated text that it is, but you have the ability to modify the Sentences to produce more natural-sounding narratives if desired.

The **Individual Narrative** report provides a narrative about a single person, based on the event Tags recorded for that person. That person's parents and children are not discussed unless the user has constructed customized Tags specifically designed to do that. If you specify multiple subjects for this report you will get individual narratives for each subject, but with no indication of how, or even if, they are related.

The **Ahnentafel** and **Descendant Indented Narrative** reports are essentially a series of individual narratives arranged in a format that indicates how the individuals are related. You specify the starting person as the Subject and the number of generations to be included, and the report then includes the ancestors or descendants for that number of generations.

The **Journal** report is intended to mimic the formats used by the major genealogical societies in their own journals. This report type includes a narrative for each person followed by a listing of that person's children. The report can be used in either Ancestor or Descendant format.

This report has a large number of options to reflect differences in the styles of the society journals and to provide features requested by users that are not included in those styles. Controlling the output of Journals starts on the General tab of Options:

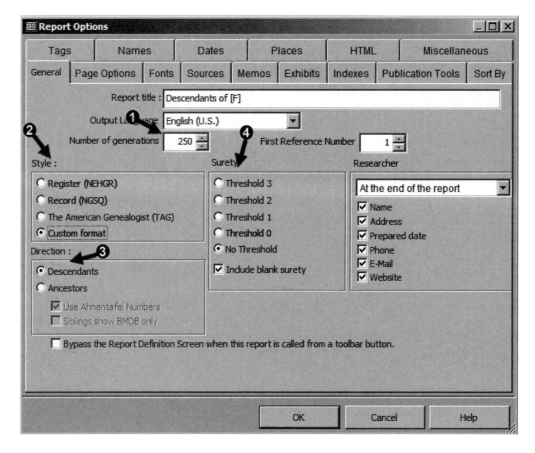

On the General tab are several of the most commonly used controls:

❶ Number of Generations – works the same for all ancestor and descendant reports.

❷ Style – is the heart of the Journal's options. Three of the well-known journals are listed. When you choose one of these Styles, a number of options on the various tabs are automatically set to produce a report similar to the style of that journal. As long as that Style is set, the associated options cannot be changed by the user, as shown on the screenshot on the facing page. Choosing the "Custom format" as shown above allows you to change any of those options, creating the exact format you choose.

❸ **Direction** – allows you to specify whether you want a Descendants or Ancestor report.

❹ **Surety** – is the often troublesome setting discussed on page 81.

When one of the journal Styles has been selected, as described in item 2, the preset options appear dimmed on the Miscellaneous screen:

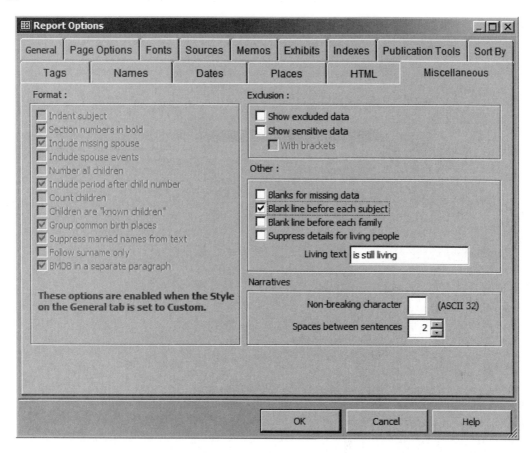

The options on the left side of the screen have been preset by choosing the Register style on the General tab and cannot be changed by the user unless the style is changed to Custom Format. Similarly, several options on the Tags and Names tabs are preset when you choose one of the three journal styles.

Forms and Charts

TMG offers a number of forms and charts, some being traditional genealogical formats and others being unique. They include the following reports:

- **Family Group Sheets** – are a traditional format used by genealogists long before the advent of computers. TMG's version offers control of contents, format, and page layout as described in the preceding sections. Note that the format produced when the report is generated as a word processor file is different than that produced to screen, printer, or as a PDF file.

- **Pedigree and Descendant Indented Charts** – are also traditional formats long used in genealogy. Because of the limited space in these formats, there is limited flexibility in specifying content, but the controls for format and page layout remain.

- **Individual Details Report** – produces a report that contains much of the data displayed on TMG's Person View. I have included it with the reports intended for sharing because it offers the same controls of content, formatting, and page layout as those reports. But most users probably consider it more of a research tool than a report that would be shared with others.

- **Relationship Chart** – is a unique report designed to display the linkage between two related people in a box-chart format. Rather than specifying "Subjects" as with the other reports, you enter the two people on the top of the Report Definition Screen. Only names and basic birth, marriage, and death information are included.

- **Kinship Report** – is another unique report, which lists the relatives of a given subject, grouped by their relationship to that person. For example, it lists spouses, parents, siblings, their spouses, nephews and nieces, their spouses, etc., continuing for the number of generations specified on the General tab of report Options.

Box Charts

TMG offers very capable tools for creating box charts, which are ancestor or descendant "trees" consisting of boxes connected by lines. There is also an "Hourglass" chart, which combines both ancestors and descendants of a starting person.

Like the other ancestor and descendant reports, you specify the starting person as Subject on the Report Definition screen and the number of generations on the General tab of report Options. The Box Charts have a special control on the Report Definition screen to include only those people with a specified Flag setting. This is useful if you want to include, say, only males, only females, or if you want to exclude specific lines from the chart.

The orientation of trees – left to right or top to bottom – for example, is controlled on the Chart Style tab of chart Options. Many aspects of the box size, line styles, and more can be controlled by the various options on the other tabs.

The process of generating Box Charts is a bit different than for other charts and reports. You set all the various options on the Report Definition screen and Options, as with the other reports. However, when you click the **Create Chart** button the information is actually transferred to a separate program that is supplied with TMG, called Visual Chartform™. If you specified the Destination of the chart as "View in Visual Chartform" Visual Chartform then opens and actually creates the chart, as shown on the facing page.

If you want to save the chart, you can so using the **File > Save** menu command in Visual Chartform.

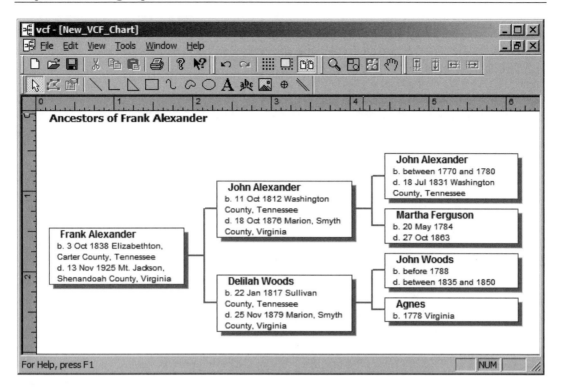

You can print your chart with Visual Chartform. If the chart is larger than a single page, you print it in sections. The **View > Page Bounds** menu command will cause the page boundaries to be displayed on screen. If boxes cross page boundaries, the chart can be reformatted to fit each box entirely on a single page with the **Tools > Diagram > Repaginate** menu command.

Wholly Genes Software offers an inexpensive high quality printing service that can print charts up to 3 feet by 25 feet. The **Report > Chart Printing Service...** menu command in TMG provides an easy way to send your completed chart for printing.

Visual Chartform is a very capable chart editor. With it you can edit the text; rearrange, add, or delete lines and boxes; and even copy one chart to another to create a completely new custom chart format. The details of this editing are beyond the scope of this guide but are covered in several of the resources listed in Appendix A – Other Resources.

If you specified the chart Designation as "Save To" a file, rather than "View in Visual Chartform," Visual Chartform creates and saves the file, but neither that program nor the chart appear on your screen. Available formats are Visual Chartform's own file format and standard bitmap and JPG image formats. The bitmap and JPG formats, as well as enhanced Metafile (emf) format, are also available from the **File > Export** menu command in Visual Chartform.

Websites

Many TMG users find that creating websites from their TMG data is very useful in three different contexts:

- **"Work-in-progress" sites** – posted as Internet websites, are primarily intended to make contact with other researchers interested in the same lines. Many users post only basic data for this purpose, along with an invitation to make contact to exchange data.

- **Family CDs** – websites shared with family members on compact disks (CDs) that are distributed to family members. This provides a way to share information with family members without posting private information on the Internet where others might find it.

- **"Share with the World" sites** – websites posted on the Internet for the purpose of sharing completed, or substantially completed, lines with anyone who is interested. These sites are generally much more complete than those intended primarily for contacting other researchers.

Websites have an advantage over paper publishing in that they are easy and inexpensive to update as new data is found, and in the case of those posted on the Internet, easy for interested researchers to find.

Many of the TMG reports can be produced in HTML – the format used for websites. This is done by specifying "Hypertext Markup Lang (HTML)" as the file type on the Report Definition screen.

Many users find the TMG reports, which were designed primarily for two-dimensional paper reports, less than ideal for website use. A program called Second Site, produced by veteran TMG user John Cardinal, is designed specifically to read TMG data files and produce web pages that are optimized for the multi-dimensional nature of websites. The program creates attractive websites "out of the box" and offers extensive features for customization for those who prefer a site tailored exactly to their own preferences.

More information about Second Site can be found on John's website: www.johncardinal.com.

Chapter 10 – Customizing Your Workspace

TMG offers a long list of features that enable the user to customize the workspace to best fit each user's preferences, experience level, computer equipment, and the specific activities being undertaken. In this chapter we discuss a number of these features and suggest when they might be useful. If you have not explored all the options available, scanning this chapter may uncover some that would be useful to you.

When you open TMG, you probably don't see this (or the color version shown on the cover):

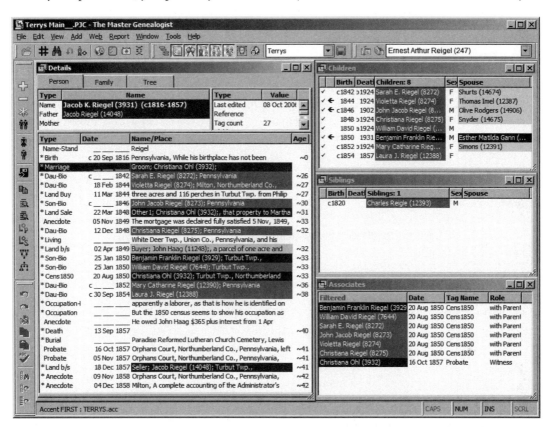

The screenshot above is similar to the way my copy of TMG usually appears. Why does your screen look different? Because I have customized my basic **Layout** to fit my preferences, work habits, and screen size; added a custom Toolbar so the functions I most commonly use are a single click away; and applied accents to color-code my ancestors, cousins, and more. A Layout is a specific arrangement of screens and Toolbars, as described further below. I'm not suggesting you would want to see the same Layout I do, but hopefully the sections that follow will suggest some ways you can make your copy of TMG work best for you.

Customizing Your Layout

You can adjust the size of the main program window on your screen if you do not want it to fill the whole screen. You can select which individual windows are displayed within the main window and set the size and position of each of them. You can adjust the widths of columns in many screens. You can select the Toolbars that will be visible and their position on the screen. Each such arrangement is called a Layout. You can save your personal Layout so it will appear when you open TMG next time. You can even save a number of different Layouts for different types of work you do and recall them when needed.

You change the various parts of Layouts as follows:

Main Window – adjust the size and position of the main window just as you do for any Windows program. If it is displayed full-screen, click the standard Windows "Restore Down" button in the upper-right corner of the screen. Then click and drag an edge or corner until it is located as you prefer.

Interior Windows – turn the individual windows on or off from the **Window** menu, or by clicking on their buttons on the Layout Toolbar. Open windows can be resized and positioned by dragging using standard Windows techniques. Note that if you let windows overlap, you cannot control which will appear on top when the Layout is reopened.

Tag Box Columns – turn on or off the columns that display Age; and the presence of Witnesses, Exhibits, Tasks, Sources, and Memos; and the maximum Surety in **Preferences > Program Options > Tag Box**. When you have the desired columns turned on you can adjust their width. Position the mouse cursor in the title bar of the columns, at the divider between two columns, until it becomes a double arrow with a vertical line between them. Then click and drag the divider to re-size the column.

Toolbars – turn Toolbars on or off and locate them along the top, bottom, or either side of the main screen or "float" them anywhere within the screen, as described on the facing page.

> Note: The various data entry screens that open and close as you work also allow you to adjust their size, position, and in some cases the width of columns. Those adjustments are automatically used next time you open that screen and are not saved as part of your Layout.

Saving a Layout

Once you have created a Layout you like, you can save it and recall it later. In fact, when you make any of the changes described above and then close the program, by default TMG will ask you whether you want to save the new layout if you have not already done so. To save a layout use the **View > Layouts > Manage Layouts** menu command.

Optional Command
Save Layout

Layout Toolbar:

You cannot modify the Standard Layout, so enter a name for your custom Layout in the field at the top of the screen and click the **Save** button. If you later want to modify your custom Layout, select it from the drop-down screen in the lower half of the screen (where "Standard" appears in the screenshot on the facing page) and click the **Overwrite** button. You can save any number of different layouts and give each a descriptive name so you can recall it easily later.

[Layout Manager dialog box]

Create a new layout using the current screen and toolbar configuration

Layout name : Terrys

Comment :

Save

Modify an existing layout

Select layout : Standard

Comment : The standard layout

Delete

Overwrite

Close   Help

The next time you open TMG, it will apply the Layout that you last saved before you closed the program.

When you first open the program, or when you save a changed layout, the name of that Layout will appear in the box in the Layout Toolbar. Adjusting the size or position of either the main window or any window inside it changes the Layout. Opening or closing any interior window is also considered a change, as is any adjustment of the Toolbars or column widths. Any change to the Layout causes the name of the current layout to disappear from the box in the Toolbar, signaling the change.

You can recall any saved Layout at any time by clicking on the drop-down arrow at the right end of the Layout Toolbar and selecting the desired layout from the list. You can also choose a saved Layout from those listed on the **View > Layouts** menu.

Customizing the Toolbars

Large with Text

TMG comes supplied with eight Toolbars to allow specific operations to be performed with just the click of a button. Only two of them, "Standard" and "Layout," are displayed in the standard Layout. You can see the others listed, and turn them on or off by either right-clicking on any Toolbar or using the **View > Toolbars** menu. I recommend turning each of the others on in turn to see if any of them seem useful to you. If so, consider making them part of your normal Layout.

Large Buttons

The buttons come in three sizes – Large with text (the default), Large,

Small Buttons

and Small. You can choose the size you prefer by right-clicking on any Toolbar, or using the **View > Toolbars** menu. Using the large buttons without text or the small buttons leaves more room for viewing your data, or room to open more Toolbars.

Toolbars can be placed at the top, bottom, or sides of the main screen or be allowed to "float" anywhere in the screen. To move a Toolbar, click and drag it by the "handle" – the small bar at the left of the screenshot below.

If you position a toolbar near the top, bottom, or a side of the main window, it automatically "docks" – that is, attaches itself to that edge. If you leave it elsewhere in the window, its appearance becomes more like a normal window, with a small title bar at the top.

All these Toolbar settings are part of the Layout, so if you want your changes to be used next time you open TMG, save the Layout as described above before closing the program.

TIP

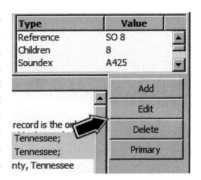

You can make more space for displaying your data by turning off the four buttons located in the right-hand side of the tag list in the Person View in **Preferences > Program Options > Data Entry**. Then turn on the Tag Editing Toolbar if it is not already part of your Layout. That Toolbar has equivalent buttons and can be located anyplace you like. Save even more space by using the keyboard for these functions. Use F4 to add a Tag, F5 to edit one, the Delete key to remove one, and the asterisk key to toggle Primary.

In addition to the eight standard Toolbars, you can create your own custom Toolbars with any buttons you find useful. In the screenshot at the beginning of this chapter, note the custom Toolbar (upper one along the left side of the screen). It contains several buttons found on various standard Toolbars, but I've added only the ones I use so those I don't need are not taking up space on my screen. I've also included some buttons not available on the standard Toolbar, such as those to switch Accents between the ones for my ancestors and for my wife's, and some for commonly used reports.

To create custom Toolbars, use the **View > Toolbars > Customize...** menu command to open the Custom Toolbar Manager. The details of that feature are beyond the scope of this guide, but clicking the **Help** button on that screen will provide detailed information about it.

Setting Fonts, Colors, Sorting and More

You can adjust the font type and sizes used in many of the individual windows and screens, as well as screen colors, and in some cases the order in which items appear, as described on the facing page.

List Fonts – many of the windows and screens are "Lists" – the Person View in the Details window, the Children and Siblings windows, the Picklist, and many other screens, such as Master Source List. You can set the font type used for these lists and the size of that font in **Preferences > Program Options > Lists**. Enter the desired size in the "Minimum font size" field. (You can set a minimum/maximum range for the font size if you choose the "TMG 5/6 method of window resizing" at **Preferences > Program Options > Other**.)

Tree and Person View Fonts – can also be set but work a bit differently. They always adjust according to the size of the screen, but you can adjust their starting point in **Preferences > Program Options > Other**. You may need to experiment with this setting a bit to get the size you like.

Prompt/Warning Font size – you can set the size of the font used in the prompt and warning screens in **Preferences > Program Options > Other**.

Screen Colors – you can set the colors for many windows and lists under **Preferences > Program Options > Colors**. By default the colors from your Windows system settings are used, but you can choose custom colors or even make each screen a different color.

Flags – you can control which Flags appear in the Flags window and the order in which they appear. To do that, right-click on the Flags window and choose **Customize Flags** to open the Flag Manager, where you can move individual Flags up or down in the list, as well as disable any you would rather not see.

List Lines – you can add vertical and horizontal lines to lists, which some users find makes them easier to read. They are controlled under **Preferences > Program Options > Lists**.

Other Info Box – at the top of the Person View displays several fields of information about the current focus person, but only the first three items are visible without scrolling. You can control the order of the items in that list and thus which are visible at the top. Right-click in that box and choose **Customize "Other Info" Box...** to set them as you prefer.

Accents

One of TMG's better features, in my opinion, is the ability to apply *Accents* to mark people with a given characteristic. The term Accent refers to color-coding the names of people when they appear in the various screens. See the screenshot at the beginning of this chapter for some examples of Accents used in the main screens, and on page 96 for examples of their use in the Picklist. Accents are a great help in seeing at a glance such things as how people are related, who has not yet been reviewed after an import or in a cleanup effort, who was born in a specific place, or any other characteristic you might find helpful.

You can choose both the text and background color for each Accent condition you define. Accent schemes can be named, saved, and later recalled, making it easy to keep several different sets of Accents for different purposes. For example, I have one that accents my wife's ancestors according to how close they are to her direct line, and a similar one for my ancestors.

Accents can be based on Flags or on any of over 1400 pre-defined **Accent Conditions**. These Accent Conditions include the number of various types of Tags; the contents of the date, place, or other fields in various Tags; the name of a parent or sibling; or whether the person is an ancestor or descendant of a specified person. The Flags used can be standard Flags, like Sex or Living, or any custom flag you might create. By creating and using custom Flags, very complex Accent systems can be defined.

TMG comes with a few prepared Accent definitions. They illustrate several useful techniques for controlling Accents:

- **Males and Females** – marks males and females with separate background colors. This example is based on the setting of the Sex Flag.

- **Living Status** – marks those with a Living status of Yes, No, or unknown with separate background colors. This example is based on the setting of the Living Flag.

- **End of Line Ancestors** – marks those whose mother and father are both unknown. This example uses the Accent Conditions "Father 'Is Not Known' " and "Mother 'Is Not Known.' "

- **Born in Virginia or Tennessee** – marks those born in either Virginia or Tennessee. This example uses the Accent Conditions "Any Birth Group tag; State" = Virginia and "Any Birth Group tag; State" = Tennessee.

The colors used in the examples demonstrate various combinations of text and background colors.

The first step in using Accents is to open the Accent Definition screen. You access that screen by one of the following:

- Using **File > Accent** menu command.

- Right-clicking on most of the main windows and choosing **Accent...** from the right-click menu.

- Using the Ctrl+A keys.

- Double-clicking on the lower-left section of the Status Bar (if you have it turned on in **Preferences > Program Options > General**).

Once in the Accent Definition screen, you can use an existing Accent definition, including the samples described above, by clicking the **Load...** button at the bottom and selecting one of the defined Accent files in the dialog box that opens. It may be helpful to Load each of the sample conditions and examine how they are defined to understand some of the methods available.

Creating a New Accent Definition

The following example shows how we might create an Accent definition that 1) marks people not yet "cleaned" after import, based on a custom Cleaned Flag (see page 16), and 2) marks with a different color all of the ancestors of a specified person.

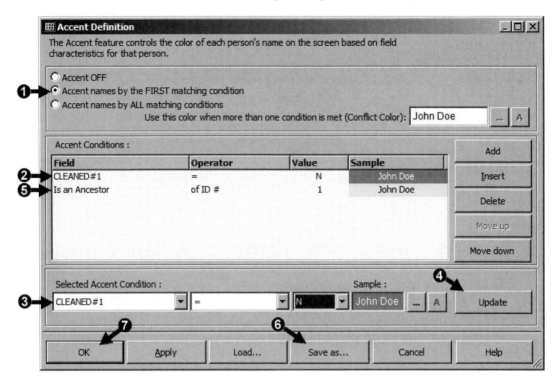

We create our new Accent definition with the following steps:

❶ Select either the second or third setting in the box at the top of the screen to turn Accents on. We selected the second setting because it makes the first condition, based on the Cleaned Flag, the dominant one, so our second condition can only be seen after the person is "cleaned."

❷ Select the first line in the "Accent Conditions" box, to modify that condition.

❸ Define the conditions for the selected line in the "Selected Accent Condition" box:

- In the Field column select the Flag Cleaned #1 from the drop-down list.

- In the Operator column select "=" from the drop-down list.

- In the Value column select N from the drop-down list.

- Click on the [...] button and select an ugly pink background in the Color screen that opens.

- Click on the **A** button and select white in the Color screen that opens.

❹ When we've defined that condition, we click the **Update** button to apply the definition we have just created to the first line.

❺ Click on the second line and similarly define the second condition. (If there is no second line, click the **Add** button to create one.) In the Selected Accent Condition box we

- Select "Is and Ancestor" and "of ID#" in the Field and Operator drop-down boxes.

- Type the target person's ID# in the Value column.

- Select background and font colors, then click the **Update** button as before.

If there are additional unneeded lines in the Accent Conditions box, select them and click the **Delete** button to remove them.

❻ Click the **Save as...** button and enter a name for this Accent Definition in the File Name field of the Save an Accent Definition File screen that opens. The name you use will appear in the Status Bar when this definition is in use.

❼ Click the **OK** button to exit the screen and apply the new definition.

When you close TMG, the Accent condition in use, if any, will be applied next time you open the program. You can recall a previously saved Accent definition by opening the Accent Definition screen and clicking the **Load...** button.

TIP

Use Flags rather than pre-defined Accent Conditions for better performance. When you define Accents based on Conditions, such as "Is an Ancestor of" some person, TMG must recompute the Condition every time you change focus from one person to another. Depending on the specific Condition used, the size of your Project, and the power of your computer system, this may result in an undesirable delay. By contrast, Accents based on Flags are much faster – TMG only has to look at the predefined Flag values for that one person. Consider creating custom Flags for Accent definitions you use often.

My Accent System – an Example

Users have developed a wide variety of Accent definitions, some for a special analysis and others to easily identify people with certain characteristics. As an example, the Accent definition I generally use has three different parts, each based on a different custom Flag:

- Cleaned – My first condition is based on my Cleaned Flag (see page 16). I place this condition first so the other conditions are not visible until the person is "cleaned," which I find is a great motivator to do some cleanup work when I'm working with a family branch that I've not looked at in some time. I also apply a very ugly pinkish shade to this Accent condition as a further motivator.

- Related By – This is based on my version of the popular "related-by" Flag, which shows how a person is related to me or to my wife. Various users have developed different versions of this Flag, which are explained on several TMG users' websites, including one on my own site – see Appendix A – Other Resources, for addresses.

- Connected – My last condition is based on my Connected Flag. It identifies people in my Project that I've not connected by blood or marriage to my family. They include persons of a surname of interest who may or may not prove to be related and neighbors and others involved with events linked to my family.

Customizing the Picklist

The Picklist is one of the more resource-intensive features – depending on the size of your Project and the capabilities of your computer system, opening and navigating it may be slower than you like. TMG addresses this by providing a choice of two styles of Picklist: Simple and Expanded. The simple version, which emphasizes speed of operation, is used by default:

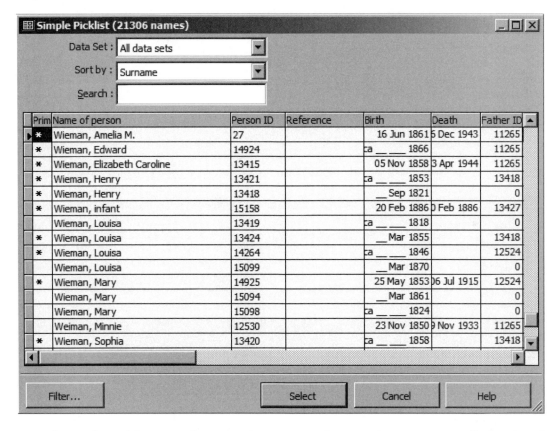

In exchange for quicker operation, you give up some features. Accents are not displayed, and you cannot specify which information is shown for each person (although you can hide a column by adjusting it to the minimum width).

The Expanded Picklist, shown on the next page, emphasizes flexibility and information in exchange for some speed of operation. You can choose it in **Preferences > Program Options > Lists**.

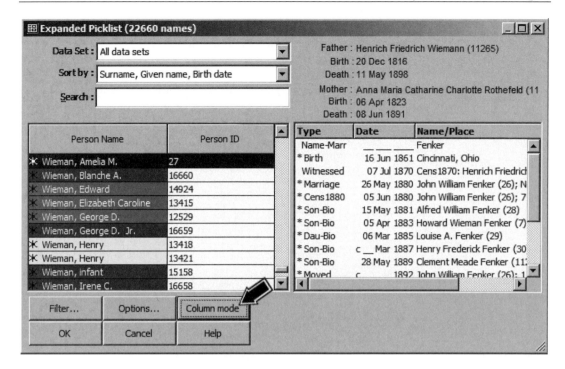

If Accents are enabled, they will appear in the Expanded Picklist (obviously, they are more useful on your color screen than in this black and white screenshot). The default Event List mode, which shows a list of events for the selected person (sort of a miniature version of the Person View), is shown above. Clicking the **Column mode** button switches to the version below:

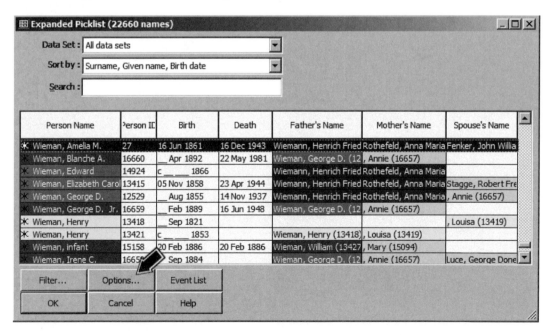

In this mode brief information about each person, including parents and last viewed spouse, is listed. You can select which columns appear by clicking on the **Options** button.

I find the column mode of the expanded Picklist to be far more useful than the default simple Picklist and suggest trying it unless the size of your Project and your available hardware make it too sluggish for comfortable use.

> Note: The Picklist is not only used to navigate from one focus person to another but can be accessed in nearly any context in which a person needs to be selected. This might be when entering a second person or Witnesses in the Tag Entry screen (see Chapter 5 – Entering and Editing Data or Chapter 12 – Witnesses). Or it could be when specifying a person in a report definition or a filter (see Chapter 8 – Reports for Research and Analysis and Chapter 9 – Genealogy Reports)
>
> To access the Picklist in these contexts, you can place the cursor in the field where the ID number is to be entered and press F2 or click the small search button that appears next to the field. After finding the name of the person you want to enter, double-click on the name to enter the person's ID number into the field.

Customizing the Add Person Screen

By default, the Add Person screen creates only the Name, Birth, and Death Tags, and if appropriate for the new person's relationship to the focus person, parent/child Relationship or Marriage Tags. You can customize the items displayed to better fit your needs:

- **Add Tag Types** – so you can create additional types of Tags as the new person is added. I often find it helpful to include the Burial and Baptism Tags, as many sources include that information. You can include any other tag you find useful.

- **Change fields** – which appear for each Tag Type. For example, you might remove Country fields if you seldom enter that field in Tags, or add sort date or Memo fields to certain tags if you commonly add them for new people.

- **Including Flags** – so they can be set for the new person. I find it useful to include the Living Flag, as well as some of my custom Flags.

To make any of these changes, click the **Setup** button in the lower left corner of the Add Person screen to open the Add Person Template screen, as shown on the next page.

You customize the Tag settings on the Tag Types tab of that screen. Those Tag Types that will appear on the Add Person Screen are listed on the left half of the screen. (The Marriage Tag appears only if the person being added was identified as the spouse of the current focus person.) Those that could be added are listed in the right half of the screen.

The options in the box in the lower part of the screen allow you to control which fields will appear in the Add Person Screen for each Tag. You can save space on that screen by omitting fields you seldom use when adding a new person.

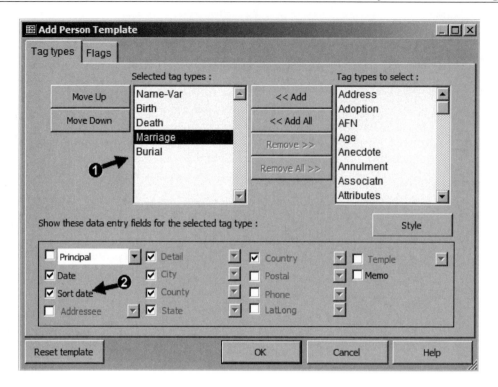

In this screenshot we have

❶ Added the Burial Tag Type by

  ▪ selecting the Burial Tag Type in the list on the right,

  ▪ clicking the **<<Add** button, and

  ▪ positioning the new tag in the list with the **Move Up** and **Move Down** buttons.

❷ Added the Sort Date field to the Marriage tag by

  ▪ selecting that Marriage Tag Type in the list on the left and

  ▪ checking "Sort date" in the lower box.

Flags are added to the Add Person screen by clicking the Flags tab and choosing and sorting them in the same way as Tag Types are selected. Adding the Living Flag, for example, allows you to manually set that Flag to N for long-dead ancestors when you do not have birth or death dates to set that Flag automatically. It is also useful if you have created custom Flags that you want to set correctly for each new person.

If you want to restore the original settings for the Add Person screen, click the **Reset Template** button.

Chapter 11 – Working with Sentences

Narrative reports are those written in complete sentences, as opposed to family group sheets, pedigrees, and other charts and forms. If you are very sure that you will never want to produce narrative output of your TMG Project in reports or a website, you can skip this chapter. In TMG, *Sentence Structures*, generally called simply Sentences, are used only to produce narrative output. All other reports and charts use different methods to assemble the data into the report format.

Sentence Structures are templates that control how the data in the various fields in Tags – names, dates, place information, or the text of memos – will be assembled into finished text when narrative reports are generated. Each Tag Type (Birth, Anecdote, Census, Marriage, Education, and so forth) has its own Sentence to generate text appropriate for the event being recorded.

The Sentence Structures supplied with the standard Tags work fine for many purposes. Still, most users of narrative reports sooner or later find that they want to modify the text generated by these standard Tags. Or they may want to create some custom Tag Types (see Chapter 14 – Adding Custom Tag Types), and find they need to create Sentence Structures so these tags will generate the desired output text. This chapter describes how to modify or create Sentences.

Local vs. Global Sentence Modifications

In working with Sentence Structures, a key point to understand is that there are two very different places where you can modify Sentences. Recall that each Tag you create in TMG is one of many Tag Types – it might be Birth, Marriage, Note, Will, or any of hundreds of others. When you change Sentences, you do it either of two ways:

Globally – by modifying the Sentence Structure of a Tag Type. This modifies the Sentence Structure for every individual Tag of that Type, both any existing Tags as well as all new Tags you may create later.

Locally – by modifying the Sentence Structure for one individual Tag. When you do that, you only change the Sentence for that one Tag.

Note: Once you make a change to the local Sentence Structure of an individual Tag, any Global changes made later to the Tag Type will *not* have any impact on that individual Tag.

Deciding to Use Local or Global Sentences, Roles, or New Tag Types

You would generally contemplate changes in a Sentence Structure because you have found that the text created by the existing Sentence is not satisfactory for some reason. It could be that you simply want to be able to include the Memo field in the output of a standard Tag Type that doesn't include it by default. Perhaps you prefer that the narrative for a certain kind of event flow in a different way. It might be that the narrative for a particular person could be improved by rearranging the text. You may have come across a type of event that is not a good fit in any existing Tag Type. Depending on the reason for the proposed change and your preferences there are several ways to approach the changes:

- If you want to add a variable to a standard Tag Type, say add the Memo to the standard Birth Tag Type so you can include details about the birth event, changing the Sentence of that Tag Type globally is a simple solution.

- If you want to change the way a specific type of event is described, say change the wording for all Census tags, the obvious approach is to modify the Sentence Structure of that Tag Type globally.

- If you find that the narrative for a particular person in your Project could be improved by rearranging the output of some Tags, it may be best to locally modify some of the Sentences of that person's Tags. Sometimes, changing the global Sentences for the Tag Types may improve the narrative for one person but make it worse for others.

- If you find that you make the same type of local changes for several but not all cases for a particular Tag Type, you may want to consider creating "Roles" for the Tag Type. See Chapter 13 – Roles, for more details on this helpful tool.

- If you have found your ancestors left records of a type of event that doesn't fit well in an existing Tag Type, there are two choices. If the type of event is found only rarely, generally the best solution is to use an existing Tag Type. You could use a very general tag type, like Note or Anecdote, and simply record the details in the Memo, or use a Tag Type designed for somewhat similar events and customize the local Sentence to better reflect your event. If there are a number of events of this type, however, it may be better to create a custom Tag Type for them (see Chapter 14 – Adding Custom Tag Types).

Where to Modify Sentence Structures

Whether you are adjusting the Sentence Structure locally for an individual Tag or globally for a Tag Type the procedure is the same – the difference is the screen you work with.

Globally – To modify the Sentence Structure of a Tag Type globally, you open the Tag Type Definition screen. To open that screen you first use the **Tools > Master Tag Type List** menu command to open the Tag Type List, which is shown in the screenshot on the facing page.

Select the Tag Type you want to edit from the list. Here we have selected the Birth Tag Type.

Optional Commands
**Open Tag Type
Definition Screen**

Tag Editing Toolbar:

Tag Entry Screen:

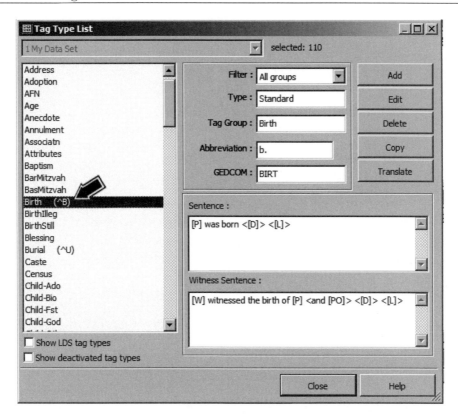

Then click the **Edit** button to open the Tag Type Definition screen:

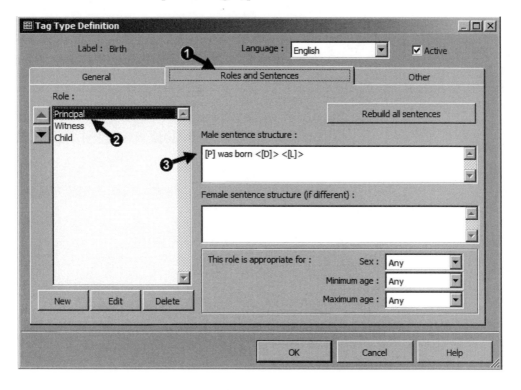

In that screen we

❶ Click on the Roles and Sentences tab.

❷ Select the Role you wish to modify in the Role list on the left side of the screen. By default, all Principals will be assigned the Role of "Principal" and all Witnesses will receive the Role of "Witness." Unless you want to explore additional Roles, these two are the only ones you need to deal with. (See Chapter 13 – Roles for more information on using other Roles.)

❸ Modify the Sentence Structure in the fields to the right in that screen. For most Tag Types only the "Male sentence structure" is used; it is applied to everyone unless there is an entry in the field labeled "Female sentence structure (if different)." The Female field is used only in those cases where different wording is required for female subjects.

A discussion on editing the Sentences is found in the section "Writing Sentence Structures" beginning on page 104.

Locally – You modify the Sentence Structure locally for an individual Tag in the Tag Entry Screen. You access that screen for an existing Tag by double-clicking on the Tag name in the Type column in the Details screen. This is also the screen you access in the course of adding a new tag.

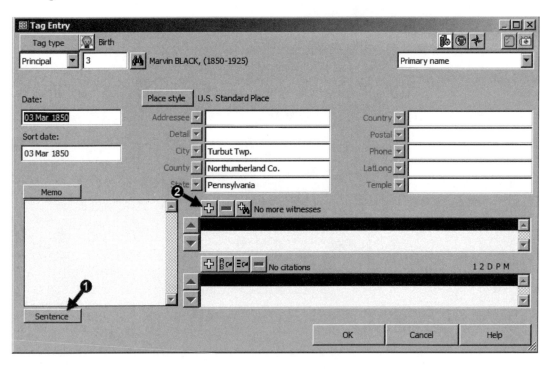

Sentence Structures for Principals and those for Witnesses are accessed from the Tag Entry screen in different ways.

❶ **Principals** – to modify the Sentence(s) for the Principal(s) at the top of the screen, click the **Sentence** button in the lower-left corner of the screen to open the Sentence Structures screen:

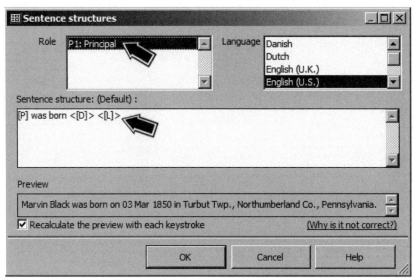

In the Role field, select the Principal you want to modify. In this case, there is only one Principal. If the Tag had two Principals, we could select either of them here.

In this view, the word "(Default)" appears after the "Sentence Structure" label, indicating that we have not yet edited the Sentence in this Tag, so the Sentence displayed is the Global Sentence Structure from the Tag Type. To change the Sentence, edit the existing text in the field below that label. Once we make changes in this field, the "Default" label will disappear.

A preview of the output appears below the Sentence Structure field. Note that the preview is an approximation of the actual output because a number of report options can affect the way the narrative appears in reports, including date formats, use of upper case for names, several options for places, and more.

❷ **Witnesses** – to modify the Sentence Structures for a new Witness click on the **+** button on Tag Entry screen. (Witnesses are discussed in Chapter 12 – Witnesses.) If you want to modify the Sentence Structure for an existing Witness, double-click on that Witness's entry in the list of Witnesses under the **+** button. Either opens the Add/Edit Witness screen, as shown on the next page.

Change the Sentence by editing the text in the Sentence Structure field. Note that when you are editing Sentences for Witnesses locally, each Witness in a Tag has his or her own Sentence, so you can customize the Sentences specifically for each Witness.

As with the Sentence Structures screen for Principals, a preview of the output appears near the bottom of the screen.

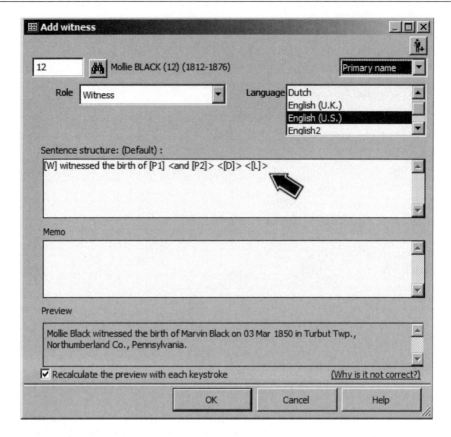

 TIP   Leave unchecked the "Recalculate the preview with each keystroke option." This avoids unexpected results in the Preview that can occur when a Sentence is partially edited, as well as any delay when editing Sentences or when typing in the Witness Memo field. When the option is unchecked a **Refresh** button appears, which you can click any time you are ready to see the updated Preview.

Writing Sentence Structures

Now that we have seen where the Sentences are changed, we need to look at the specific changes we might make. To determine how you want to change the existing Sentence, you must first decide exactly how you want the text in the report to read. Only then can you begin to craft the new or revised Sentence itself.

Looking at the existing Sentence may offer clues. For example, look at the standard Sentence Structure for the Birth Tag, visible in the "Sentence Structure" screenshot on the preceding page:

[P] was born <[D]> <[L]>

The letters in square brackets are *Variables*. Variables refer to items recorded in various fields of the Tag and indicate were they will be placed in the finished text.

- [P] stands for "Principal" – the person whose ID Number is entered in the upper-left corner of the screen. This Variable will cause either the name of that person to be printed, or if this is not the first sentence of the report paragraph, the pronoun "he" or "she."

- [D] stands for "Date" – the date entered in the Tag's Date field. The Date format is controlled by settings in the Report Definition for the particular report being generated, and in **Preferences > Program Options > General**.

- [L] stands for "pLace" – the information entered in the several Place fields on the Tag. The Report Definition settings control how the place information is formatted.

A full list of available Sentence Variables can be found by searching Help for "Variables." Then look for "Variables (Event tags)" in the list that is produced. You can simply type variables in the Sentence Structure field. Or click the spot where you want the variable to be inserted, right-click, and choose the desired Variable from the pop-up menu, as shown in the screenshot below, where the full Memo variable, [M], has been selected.

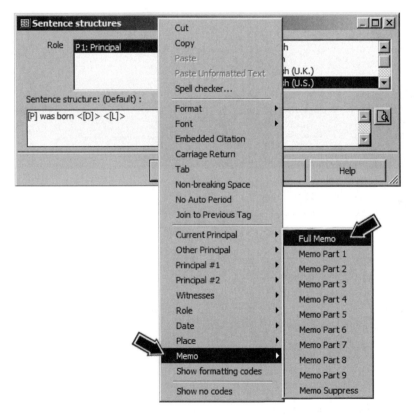

The angle brackets around some variables – such as "<[D]>" in the Birth Tag Sentence – are called ***Conditional Brackets***. They tell the program to simply ignore whatever is included between them if the field referenced by the variable is empty. If these brackets are omitted and the indicated field is empty, a phrase like "an unknown value" appears in the text in place of the missing data.

The punctuation marks and any text – such as "was born" in the Birth Tag Sentence – will appear in reports exactly as they are written in the Sentence Structure.

The screenshot below shows the result of a simple change to the global Sentence of the standard Birth Tag Type.

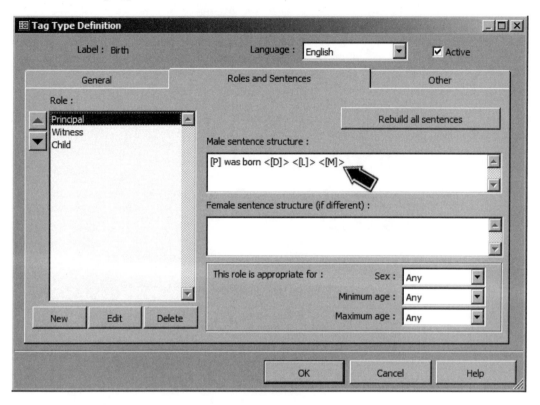

Here the Variable for the Memo field, [M], has been added to the Sentence, allowing us to record any details we might want to include about the birth. We might want to add something like "on the voyage to New York," for example. Note that the Variable has been included in Conditional Brackets. We did that so when nothing is entered in the Memo field the added Variable will be ignored, but for those cases where we do include a remark in the Memo field that text will be included in the narrative automatically. Use of Conditional Brackets is generally a good idea when adding Variables globally. These added Variables often represent fields used in some Tags but not others, and with the Conditional Brackets the Sentence works well in either case.

Testing Your Work

Especially as you first start working with Sentences, it is a good idea to verify that you have obtained the results you had in mind by testing your newly modified Sentence with some real data. If you are modifying a local Sentence – that is, the Sentence in an individual Tag – a preview appears on the Sentences Structures screen, as described on page 103. You can see a good approximation of your result there. For a final test using the options you generally specify in reports, run a test report, which also lets you see the output of the Tag in the context of surrounding Tags. This is especially useful if you are trying to "fine tune" the narrative for an individual to make it read as you like. TMG has a button on the Reports Toolbar that creates a preview report in the Individual Narrative format.

If you want to test your work for a global Sentence Structure – that is, one in the Tag Type – you will need to find a Tag of that Type being used for a person because TMG needs some actual data to create a preview. A good way to do that is to find a person who has a Tag of the Type you want to modify (one whose Sentence has not been modified locally), and then

- Open the Tag Entry screen for that Tag.

- Click the **Sentence** button to open the Sentence Structures screen, and use the preview screen there to check your work.

If the results are not as you expect, return to the Tag Type Definition screen, edit the Sentence, and test again.

TIP

Rather than switching back and forth between screens to test a global Sentence that did not work as expected, make the necessary changes in the Sentence of the Tag you are using as a test. When the Preview has verified that it works as expected, copy the Sentence in the Tag, go to the Tag Type Definition screen for the Tag Type, and paste it into the Sentence Structure there. Your tested Sentence then becomes the global Sentence for the Tag Type.

Some General Considerations

Experimenting with global changes to Sentences is relatively safe, at least until you start "polishing" the narratives of selected people, because you can simply change them again. Doing so is a good way to learn about how Sentence Structures work.

Once you reach the point of wanting more polished narratives, at least for some people in your Project, in my opinion the best tool is to locally modify the Sentences of selected Tags for those people. Especially for people for whom you have considerable information, producing quality text requires hand-crafting of the narrative. Using local Sentences in key Tags is essential, I believe, in achieving that.

Some users prefer to leave the global Sentences and edit the finished narrative in a word processor. If you expect to produce finished narrative only once for a given line, as a professional researcher might, that may work well. However, I find I continually produce narrative reports for cousins, or web pages with Second Site, each including a different group of people but often containing many of the same ones. I see no need to continually polish the narratives for the same people time and again when I can make those changes in TMG and have them reflected each time that person appears in a report or web page.

Chapter 12 – Witnesses

One of TMG's more useful features, and one that may be unique among genealogy programs, is the ability to record an unlimited number of people who were associated with an event. For example, the Witness feature allows you to include in a single Tag any of the following:

- All the members of a household in a census.

- Family members who immigrated together.

- The executors and heirs named in a will.

- The minister and attendants at a wedding.

- The pallbearers in a funeral.

As we saw in Chapter 5 – Entering and Editing Data, most Tags allow one to enter two Principals. Those are the one or two people most intimately involved in the event. Any number of other people can be attached to the Tag as *Witnesses*. A Witness in TMG is simply one who has any association with the event. They are not necessarily eyewitnesses, nor even witnesses in a legal sense, such as one who witnessed the signing of a will. The association with the event can be quite indirect. For example, some users add spouses or children as Witnesses to a Death Tag, not because they were present at the death, but to report that the spouse was widowed or the children were orphaned.

The Witness feature is not available when operating in the Beginner Data Entry mode. See page 43 for use of the Advanced Data Entry Mode, which makes Witnesses visible on the screens.

Why Add Witnesses?

In its simplest application, using Witnesses saves entering redundant information in multiple Tags. For example, you might create a census Tag with the head of household as Principal and add all the other members of the household as Witnesses. Doing so causes that tag to appear in the Person View of each member of the household, and optionally in reports about them. You only have to enter the date, place, any memo text, and the citation once instead of for each person.

The Associates window can display all the Principals and/or Witnesses present in all the Tags for the current Focus Person, so it is easy to see all the other people you have associated with that person. You can quickly navigate to any of them by double-clicking on their names in the Associates window.

But Witnesses are much more powerful than that. Once we have added the members of a census household as Witnesses, we can modify the Sentences of the Principals, or even of the Witnesses, so that narrative reports about one person can include mention of the names of any or all of the others involved in the event. For example, the narrative about a parent can mention all the children in the household in a census, or children who immigrated with their parents. The narrative about the marriage of a couple can mention the pastor and all the attendants if you like.

Basic Functions of Witnesses

Simply attaching a Witness to an event Tag accomplishes the most basic functions of Witnesses – the ability to enter the details of an event only once and have that Tag appear for participants beyond the one or two Principals. It also displays a linkage between the participants in the Person View and Associates windows. When used with the default settings for the standard Tag Types, attaching a Witness causes the following results:

- In the Person View of the person entered as Witness, the Tag will appear in the list of Tags. The label in the Type column will be "Witness." The Tag Type and name of the Principal(s) will appear in the Name/Place column.

- The Witness, identified as "Witness," appears in the Associates window when either of the Principals of the Tag are the Focus Person.

- The Tag will appear in the Family Group Sheet and Individual Detail reports for the Witness, identified as "Witness." The Tag Type and names of the Principals will be displayed. The Witness will not appear in reports for the people entered as Principals.

- For most Tag Types, in the section in narrative reports for the Witness there will be a statement similar to "He witnessed the birth of John Jones…." The Witness will not be mentioned in the sections of the report about the Principals.

- For certain Tag Types, including those in which entering Witnesses is most useful, the output is tailored to their specific application. For example, when a Witness is entered in a Census Tag, the output will be something like "He appeared on the census of 1850 in the household of John Jones and Mary Smith…." Emigration, Employment, Occupation, Pagr List (Passenger List), Religion, and Residence Tags produce similarly tailored output for Witnesses. In each case, the Witness will not appear in the report sections for the Principals.

As this list shows, the Witness feature can be quite useful with only the default Sentence Structures. Given all the power and flexibility of the feature, it should come as no surprise that one can obtain more than these basic results with a bit more effort on the part of the user, as described in the following sections.

TIP
The Associates window is not part of the standard Layout and is not particularly useful if you are not using Witnesses. But if you are using Witnesses, it can be very useful, displaying all the people you have associated with the current Focus Person. You can quickly change the focus to any Witness by double-clicking on his or her name in the Associates window. You can open the Associates window with the **Window > Associates** menu command. If you find it useful, you can make it a part of your Layout as described in Chapter 10 – Customizing Your Workspace.

Adding Household Members to the Narratives of Principals

One very useful application of Witnesses is to name, in the narratives about the Principals, other participants in an event. This can be done by modifying the standard Sentences for the Principals (Sentences are described in Chapter 11 – Working with Sentences). The following example, using a Census tag, demonstrates how that can be done.

The default Sentence for Principals in the Census Tag is

[P] <|and [PO]> appeared on the census <of [D]> <[L]>

This produces text in narrative reports similar to

John Jones and Mary Smith appeared on the census of 1850 in Lyon Co., Kentucky.

If the other members of the household are attached to the Census Tag as Witnesses, they do not appear in the narratives for the Principals, but that can be changed by editing the Sentence for the Principals to something like the following:

[P] <|and [PO]> appeared on the census <of [D]> <[L]> <, with [WO] also listed in the household>

This would produce text in narrative reports similar to

John Jones and Mary Smith appeared on the census of 1850 in Lyon Co., Kentucky, with Johnnie Jones, Mary Jones, and Sarah Jones also listed in the household.

This same approach would work well for Emigration, Passenger List, and Residence Tags, for example, allowing all the family members to be listed together in the parents' narratives.

The changes suggested above could be made locally, in the individual Tags, but it is generally more convenient to make this type of change globally, in the Tag Type. Just be sure to include the conditional brackets (angle brackets) as shown in the example above so that the Sentence works equally well whether or not there are Witnesses present in the Tag. Failure to include the conditional brackets will result in output like the following if there are no Witnesses present:

John Jones and Mary Smith appeared on the census of 1850 in Lyon Co. Kentucky, with an unknown person also listed in the household.

Modifying Sentences globally is described on page 100.

Witnesses with Different Parts in the Event

Sometimes we want to record several participants in an event as Witnesses, but they played different parts in the event. We can do that by modifying the Sentence Structure for each

Witness so that the narratives do reflect each Witness's unique part. The following example, using a Will tag, demonstrates how that can be done:

The default Sentence for Witnesses in the Will Tag is

[W] witnessed the will of [P] <and [PO]> <[D]> <[L]>

This produces text in narrative reports something like

He witnessed the will of Tom Jones on 3 Jul 1850.

This is fine if the Witness was literally a witness; that is, he witnessed the Principal sign the will. However, we might want to record as Witnesses the Executor and the Heir, instead of or in addition to those who witnessed the signing of the document. We can do that by editing the Witness Sentence so it reads something like one of the following:

[W] was named an executor in the will of [P] <and [PO]> <[D]> <[L]>

[W] was named an heir in the will of [P] <and [PO]> <[D]> <[L]>

These would produce text in narrative reports something like

He was named an executor in the will of Tom Jones on 3 Jul 1850.

He was named an heir in the will of Tom Jones on 3 Jul 1850.

These changes to the Sentence Structures would be made locally, in each Tag, and separately for each Witness. While you could change the Witness Sentence globally for the Will Tag Type so that it says "heir" instead of "Witness," you cannot create two different parts, say both "executor" and "heir" by this method in the Tag Type – you have to use Roles to do that, as discussed in the next chapter. Modifying Sentences locally is described on page 102.

For the narratives of the Principals, this method does not allow you to specify different parts for specific Witnesses. That can be done by typing the names of the Witnesses, along with their parts into the Memo, but it is easier to do it by the use of Roles, which are discussed in the next chapter.

Entering Witnesses

To add Witnesses to a Tag, we open the Tag Entry Screen, as seen in the screenshot on the next page. In this example, we are entering in a Will Tag a person who witnessed the signing of a will.

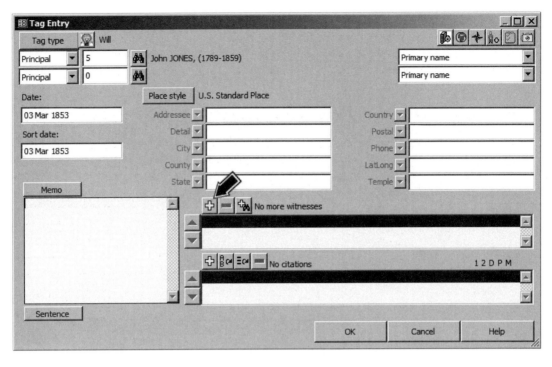

Click the **+** button to open the Add Witness Screen:

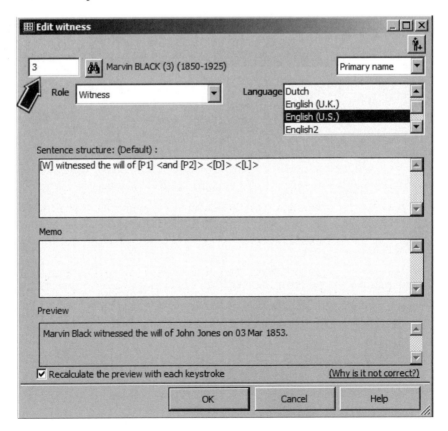

We enter the Witness's ID number in the field in the upper left corner of the screen, if we recall it, or we can click the binoculars button and select the person with the Picklist. When we move the cursor to another field, the person's name appears next to the binoculars button. We could modify the Witness Sentence, but it's unnecessary in this case, so we click **OK** to close the Add Witness screen and return to the Tag Entry Screen:

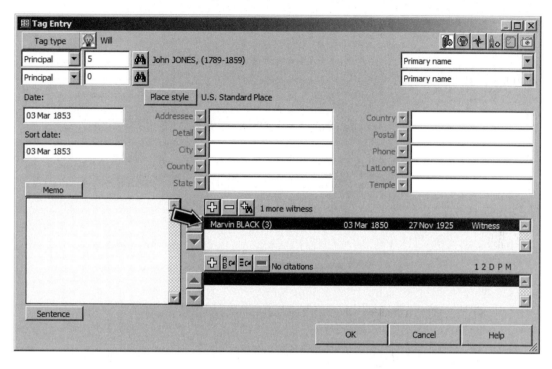

We see that the Witness now appears in the list of Witnesses. If we want to add more witnesses, we click the **+** button again and repeat the process for each one.

Witness Memos

The Memo screen visible at the lower half of the Edit Witness screenshot on the facing page is called the ***Witness Memo***. It is a memo field intended to record notes specific to that Witness. For example, in a Will Tag in which we enter heirs as Witnesses, we might enter details about the property bequeathed to each heir in their respective Witness Memos.

Witness Memos are not used by any of the default Sentence Structures, but can be included by adding the Variable [WM] to the Sentence Structure for the Witness. Witness Memos cannot be included in the Sentences for Principals, nor can the Witness Memo for one Witness be referred to in the Sentence for another Witness.

Chapter 13 – Roles

The **Roles** feature in TMG is a powerful tool for recognizing the various parts individuals played in an event. Roles are a means to specify a person's part in an event and cause screens and reports to reflect that part. In a Marriage tag, for example, one might have persons with the Roles of Bride, Groom, Minister, Maid of Honor, Best Man, and many more.

TMG's Standard Roles

Whether the user notices or not, every person entered in TMG is assigned a Role in every Tag in which they are entered. By default, every person entered as a Principal in a tag is assigned the Role "Principal." Every person entered as a Witness is assigned the Role "Witness."

Some standard tags offer additional Roles. For example, the marriage tag offers the Roles of "Bride" and "Groom," the Birth tag offers the Role of "Child," and the Death tag offers "Deceased." There is little point in applying these standard Roles, because in every case the Sentence Structure for the Role is the same as for the Principal Role in that Tag, so use of these Roles has no effect in narrative reports. However, some users apply them in order to see the Role labels on the screens.

What Can Roles Do?

Roles provide four separate, but related, functions:

- **Apply descriptive labeling** about the person's part in events in the Person View, the Associates window, and in Family Group Sheet and Individual Narrative reports.

- **Create appropriate text** in narrative reports for the participants playing each part. For example, in a Will Tag, the narrative about the testator would say he or she wrote the will, while the narratives for the executor and the heirs will say they were named executor or heirs, etc.

- **Allow reference by Role name** for each group of participants in the narratives about the others. For example, in a Will Tag, the narrative about the testator might say that he "named the following persons as heirs" and then name them. It might also say that others were witnesses and name them. Likewise, in the narratives about the other participants, such Roles make it easy to create Sentence Structures for one participant that correctly refer to other participants, something difficult to do without the use of Roles.

- **Allow you to create a "library"** of Sentence Structures within a single Tag Type. When you create a Tag to record an event, you can simply choose an appropriate Role for each participant, and the narrative output correctly describes that participant's role in the event. For example, in a Marriage Tag you can create different Sentences for first, second, and third marriages and select the appropriate one by choosing a Role.

When you use Roles, you might use any or all of these functions. But it helps to understand that they are separate, so we can apply them to achieve the results we expect.

Overview

Recall that Roles define the parts played by participants in an event. TMG offers separate Tag Types to record different types of events – birth, marriage, death, writing of a will, military service, etc. Roles are defined for each Tag Type, so each Tag Type can have different Roles suited for recording the type of event for which the Tag Type was designed. The use of Roles is a two-part process:

- **Define Roles for a Tag Type** – before you can use Roles, you have to define them for the Tag Type in which you want to use them. You might do this for an existing Tag Type, to improve its functioning, or in a new custom Tag Type you create.

  When you create Roles in a Tag Type, you define a global Sentence Structure for that Role. That Sentence defines how participants assigned the Role will be described in narrative reports about them.

  If you choose, you can modify the Sentence Structures of other Roles so the Sentences refer to various participants by Role. This is not required but can be a powerful tool in certain applications, as we will see later.

- **Apply the Role in a Tag** – once the Roles are defined for a Tag Type, the Roles must be applied to persons entered as Principals or as Witnesses in individual Tags in order to take effect. You can make this assignment for new Tags you create, or you might edit existing Tags to change the Roles for participants already entered.

Using Roles – An Example

We will use a simple case as an example – a Will Tag. The Tag will record information about the will, from the perspective of four different sets of people involved:

1. The **Testator**, who wrote the will.
2. The **Witnesses**, who witnessed the signing of the will.
3. The **Executor**, who was named to oversee the execution of the will after the death of the Testator.
4. The **Heirs**, who were named to receive the proceeds of the estate.

We will create a Will Tag that records all of these participants and correctly describes their roles when we create narrative reports about them. We plan to enter the testator as the only Principal in the Tag. All the others will be entered in the Tag as Witnesses.

Creating Custom Roles

In this example, we start with the standard Will Tag Type and add several custom Roles. The example will demonstrate several different applications of Roles.

Once we have decided that a Role would be useful for a particular Tag Type, we begin by editing that Tag Type to add the desired Role. Use the **Tools > Master Tag Type** menu command to open the Master Tag Type list, and select the Tag Type you want to edit (or we could create a new Tag Type as defined in Chapter 14 – Adding Custom Tag Types).

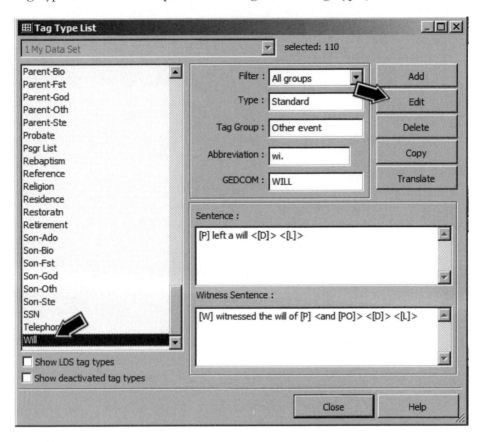

After selecting the Tag Type to be used, click the **Edit** button to open the Tag Type Definition Screen, as shown in the screenshot on the facing page. On that screen, we click the Roles and Sentences tab.

In the list on the left side of the screen, you can see all the existing Roles in this Tag Type. In this case there are only the two default Roles, "Principal" and "Witness." To add a new Role, click the **New** button below the list of Roles. This opens the New Role screen, as shown in the second screenshot on the next page. In that screen, we type in the name of our new Role.

In this example we will add two custom Roles, "Heir" and "Executor." We could create a custom Role for the testator, but there is no need since we intend that the only Principal in the Tag will be the person who wrote the will. I see no value in creating custom roles when the standard ones will serve just as well. Likewise, the standard Witness Role will serve very well for the witnesses to the signing of the will.

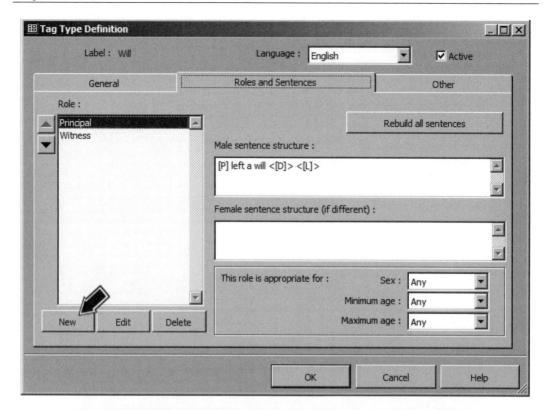

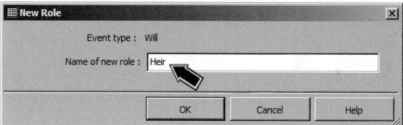

Defining Role Sentences

Once the new Roles have been created, we need to create appropriate Sentence Structures for them. This is done on the Roles and Sentences tab of the Tag Type Definition Screen, as shown on the following page.

We select a Role we want to modify, and edit the Sentence Structure for that Role (see Chapter 11 – Working with Sentences). Here we have entered the Sentence Structure for the "Heir" role:

[W] was named an heir in the will of [P] < dated [D]> <[L]><[MO]>

Note: The variable <[MO]> is a code indicating that the contents of the Memo field are not to be included even if the report option to include Memos is used.

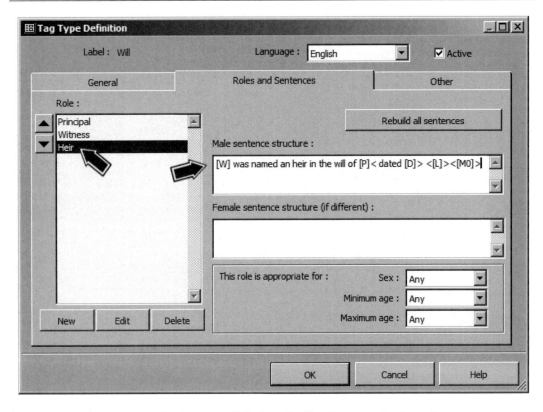

We would similarly create the "Executor" Role and add a Sentence for it, perhaps

[W] was named an executor in the will of [P] < dated [D]> <[L]><[M0]>

Since the term "executor" is gender specific, we might also create a female Sentence for it, something like

[W] was named an executrix in the will of [P]< dated [D]> <[L]><[M0]>

These Sentences will be used in the narrative for each participant, to describe their participation. For example, if we create a narrative about the executor of this will, it might read

He was named an executor in the will of John Jones dated 3 Mar 1853.

We could modify the Sentences for the Principal (testator) and Witness Roles, but the default Sentences are really adequate.

If all we want to do is create text that properly describes the role of each participant in the event, our task is done. We can skip to applying the Roles we have defined, but we might want to use the more complex feature of using Roles to refer to participants to enhance the Sentence for the Principal, as described in the next section.

Using Role Names to Refer to Participants by Role

One of the more useful features of Roles is the ability to refer to other participants by role. We will apply this feature to enhance the narrative for the testator by listing the witnesses, executor, and heirs. We select the "Principal" Role, since that is the one we are using for the testator, and modify the Sentence for that Role.

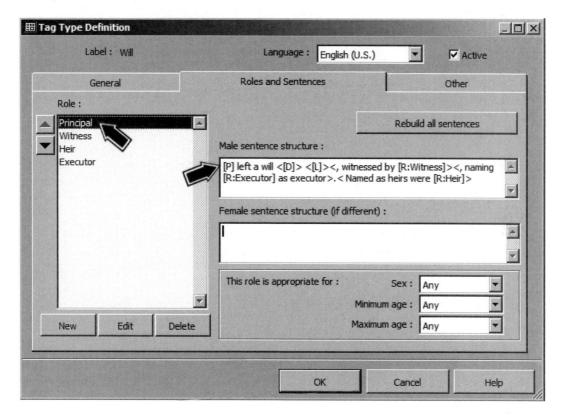

We have entered the following Sentence:

> [P] left a will <[D]> <[L]><, witnessed by [R:Witness]><, naming [R:Executor] as executor>.< Named as heirs were [R:Heir]>

Note that the Role name variables are used to refer to each group of participants by role, with appropriate wording to identify them. The narrative produced by the Sentence illustrated here might be something like

> He left a will 3 Mar 1853, witnessed by Marvin Black and George White, naming Robert Jones as executor. Named as heirs were Mary Jones, Robert Jones, and Martha Evens.

Some notes on the Role name variables used here:

- The Role variables contain two parts. The part before the colon, just "R" here, tells what output the variable will produce. The second part, after the colon, is the name of the Role itself.

- Some Role variables commonly used are:

Variable	Output	Example
[R:*Rolename*]	full name	Robert Lee Jones
[RF:*Rolename*]	first name	Robert
[RG:*Rolename*]	given name	Robert Lee

  There are a number of other variables available. To review them, search Help for "Variables," select "Variables (Event Tags)," and in that Help article, scroll three-quarters of the way to the bottom for the section on "Roles."

- If there is more than one person with the specified Role, as is the case with the "Witness" and "Heir" Roles here, the name variables produce a list of all the participants with that role.

- A careful observer will note that the Sentence in this example will have difficulty with certain combinations of participants. For example, having only one Heir or having more than one Executor, will produce an awkward result. It is possible to create more complex Sentences that will deal with such cases, but that is beyond the scope of this example. Alternatively, one can edit the Sentences locally in individual Tags to deal with such cases.

Applying the Roles

Once we have defined the Roles in the Tag Type, we are ready to apply them. We do this by editing an existing Tag of that type, or by creating a new one. Open the Tag Entry screen and enter each of the participants, assigning them each the appropriate Role. The results are shown in the screenshot on the facing page.

In this example, we entered the testator as Principal and left him with the default Role of "Principal." If we had wanted to assign to him a different Role, we would have used the drop-down list to the left of the Principal's ID number, just below the **Tag Type** button.

All the other participants are entered as Witnesses and assigned their appropriate Roles. For those entered as Witnesses, the Roles are assigned with the Roles drop-down list in the Add/Edit Witness screen, as shown in the second screenshot on the facing page. That screen is opened by clicking the + button above the Witnesses list to add a new Witness, or by double-clicking the name of an existing Witness in the list.

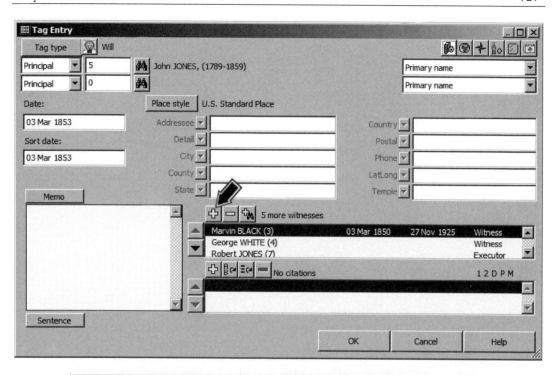

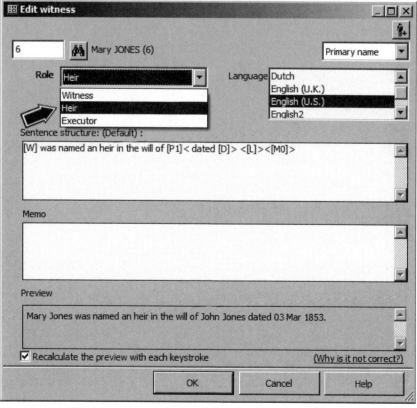

Assigning a Role to the Witness automatically assigns the Sentence Structure from that Role so that participant is correctly described in his or her own narrative.

Some Thoughts on Design of Roles

Giving some forethought to exactly how you intend to use the Roles before you create them can improve the chances of quickly obtaining your desired results. The following points may help in designing custom Roles:

- The default "Principal" Role is automatically applied to each person entered in a Tag as a Principal. The default "Witness" Role is automatically applied to each person entered in a Tag as a Witness.

- You cannot apply the "Principal" Role to those entered as Witnesses, nor the "Witness" Role to those entered as Principals.

- Other than the "Principal" and "Witness" Roles, you can apply any Role, to any person entered in the Tag, both those entered as Principals and those entered as Witnesses.

- When there are two Principals entered in a Tag, if one is assigned any Role other than the default "Principal" Role, the other must be assigned another Role as well.

- In designing a custom Role, I find it a good practice to decide whether the Role will be assigned to people entered as Principals or Witnesses. Trying to create Roles that can be used for both complicates the design of Sentences and precludes use of some helpful techniques.

- One can use the Role name variables within the Sentences for a Role to refer to the participant with that Role. For example, we might use [R:Heir] here instead of [W] to refer to this heir. There is generally no need to do that, and typing in the longer variables seems to me to invite errors. I recommend using [W] for Roles to be used for Witnesses and [P] for Roles for Principals unless there is a specific reason to do something else.

The Confusing Term "Witness"

In this example, we use the term "witness" in two different ways. TMG uses the term "Witness" to describe any participant in an event. One or two of them are also called "Principals" and are entered in the upper-left corner of the Tag Entry screen. Everyone else is called an "Other Witness," or more commonly, just a "Witness." The Other Witnesses are entered in the Witness area of the Tag Entry screen, as shown in the outlined box below in the screenshot on the next page.

People entered as Witnesses may be witnesses in the ordinary sense, meaning they witnessed the event, such as our witnesses to the signing of the will. They may be associated with the event in another way, such as our executor or heirs. In the screenshot on the next page, we see five people entered as Other Witnesses in TMG terms, meaning they are not Principals (there is one Principal in this example, entered at the top left of the screen). Of the Other Witnesses, only the first two are assigned the Role of "Witness," meaning that they actually witnessed the signing of the will. A third Other Witness is assigned the Role of "Executor." Two more persons entered as Other Witnesses are assigned the Role of "Heir." Note the label "5 more witnesses" above the Witness field, which tells us that five persons have been entered as Other Witnesses ("more" meaning in addition to the Principals).

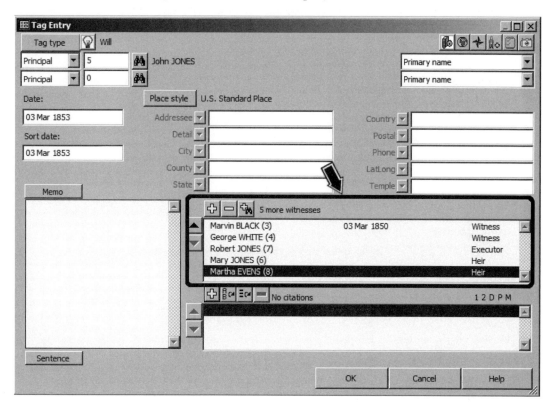

More About Using Roles

The discussion of Roles in this chapter is necessarily limited to some general concepts. For examples of other applications, including some that are much more complex, see the sources listed in Appendix A – Other Resources.

Chapter 14 – Adding Custom Tag Types

As we have seen, in TMG virtually all information about a person is placed in Tags. There are over 100 standard Tag Types, designed to accommodate a wide variety of data. There are also several general-purpose ones like Anecdote and Note that can be used when there is no specific Tag Type that is suitable for the particular case.

Even with this broad selection available, many users find it helpful to create a few custom Tag Types, either to accommodate special types of information that is encountered in their research, or to better control how TMG manages their data. This chapter describes how to create such custom Tag Types.

Why Create a Custom Tag Type?

There seems to be little point in creating a custom Tag Type for an unusual type of event that occurs only once or twice in your data. It would be better to either use a generic Tag Type like Anecdote or Note, or modify the Sentence locally in a Tag of the best fitting standard Tag Type. Still, there are several good reasons to create custom Tag Types. They include

- Providing an easy way to record events that occur with reasonable frequency and are not easily accommodated with any of the standard Tag Types.

- Providing easy-to-find labels for Tags recording unusual events in the Person View or in Family Group Sheet or Individual Detail reports.

- Allowing certain types of events to be easily excluded from reports when desired.

- Dealing with names or relationships in a way not accommodated by the standard Tag Types.

There are some specific situations where custom tag types are particularly useful:

- **Alternate Data** – create "-alt" versions of common Tag Types to record alternate data from conflicting sources. See page 27 for discussion of this usage. The most commonly used "-alt" Tag Types are Birth-alt, Marriage-alt, and Death-alt.

- **Census Years** – many users prefer to have a separate Tag Type for each census year, with the year as part of the Tag Type label. This makes it easy to see by a glance at the Person View whether that person has been found in all expected censuses. It also allows customizing the narrative output for each census year.

- **Restricted Data** – used when you record information that you may not want to include in reports, or may only want to include in some reports. For example, you may have an anecdote about someone that you may only want to include in reports you will send to selected people. If you place that information in a standard Anecdote Tag, it is more difficult to restrict its inclusion without also excluding other data in Anecdote Tags. If you use a custom Tag Type, say "Story," you can choose to include or exclude that Tag Type in any given report. (See page 80 discussion of how to select Tag Types in reports.)

- **"Not Married" Couples** – users with a number of couples in their data who had significant relationships but were not married sometimes create a custom Tag Type called "Liaison," "Partners," or the like to record a relationship other than a formal marriage.

- **Standardized Names** – those with ancestors that changed the spelling of their surnames several times sometimes find it difficult to find a particular person in their Project when they cannot recall which spelling was used by a particular generation. By adding to each person who used an alternate spelling a Name-Standard tag with a standardized spelling, the person can be found by that spelling regardless of the spelling used in the primary Name Tag. Generally this Tag Type would be omitted from reports.

Creating a Custom Tag Type

Tag Types are created by using the **Tools > Master Tag Type List** menu command to open the Master Tag Type List. On that screen, click the **Add** button to open the Tag Type Definition screen:

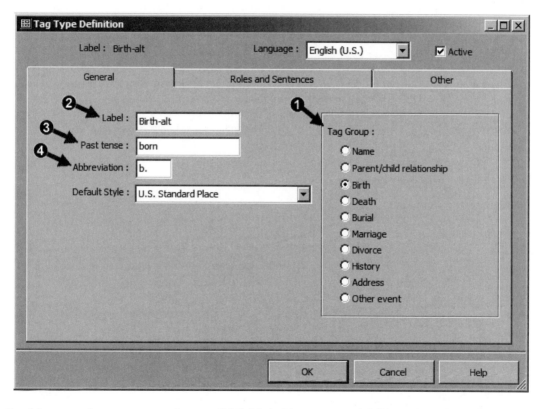

In this example, we are creating an "alt" birth Tag to record information about births that conflicts with data from other sources. We complete four entries on the General tab:

❶ **Tag Group** – is probably the most often missed entry. By default, the new Tag Type is assigned the same group as the Tag Type that was selected when we clicked **Add** in the Master Tag Type List. If we select an incorrect group the Tags we create will not function as we expect. For example, custom name Tags must be in the Name group, or you cannot create a functioning name with them. Tags in the Birth, Marriage, Death, and Burial groups all have special functions and are treated in special ways in various reports.

In this case we choose the Birth group. We want our custom Tag to be in the Birth group so we can change a Birth-alt Tag to a regular Birth Tag, and the reverse. We might want to do that if we later decide that the data we entered in a Birth-alt Tag is, in fact, more likely correct than what we have entered in the regular Birth Tag. You cannot change an existing Tag of one type to another type unless they are in the same group.

> Note: It is important that the correct group be selected before you click **OK** because the group cannot be changed after the Tag Type is created. Changing the group after the Tag Type is created requires deleting that Tag Type and creating a new one. All fields other than the group can be edited later if desired.

❷ **Label** – can be whatever we want, but consider that it will be listed alphabetically in the Tag Type List when we add a new Tag, and we want to be able to find it easily. The Label also appears in the Type column of the Person view when a Tag of this type is created, so we want the label to be meaningful but not too long to fit in that column. Finally, the Label appears in the Family Group Sheet and Individual Detail reports, so we want it to be meaningful there. Here we have entered "Birth-alt" as the Label.

❸ **Past Tense** – is used in the list of children in the Journal report to create the brief statement about the child's events. We have entered "born" as the Past tense.

❹ **Abbreviation** – is used to identify the Tag in charts such as the Pedigree, where space is limited. We have entered "b." as the Abbreviation.

Adding Roles and Sentences

If you are sure you will never want to create narrative style reports, you can ignore the Roles and Sentences tab of the Tag Type Definition. But if you think you might want to eventually use that report style, it is good to create Sentences for your custom Tag Type. By establishing the Sentence initially, as you create Tags of this type you can enter data that will produce the expected output. (You must be using the Advanced Data Entry mode to use Sentences.)

Sentences and Roles are entered on the Sentences and Roles tab of the Tag Type Definition screen, as shown in the screenshot on the facing page.

First, we make sure the Principal Role is selected, and enter a Sentence for the Principal. Generally, there is no need for a separate Female Sentence, but if we were using any words that would be different for males and females, such as "he" and "she" or "executor" and "executrix," we would also enter a Female Sentence. (See Chapter 11 – Working with Sentences, for information on how to construct Sentences.)

In this case we do not intend to use the Witness feature for this Tag Type, so we do not create a Sentence for that Role. If we did plan to enter Witnesses, we would select Witness in the Role list and also enter a Sentence for Witnesses. (Witnesses are discussed in Chapter 12 – Witnesses.)

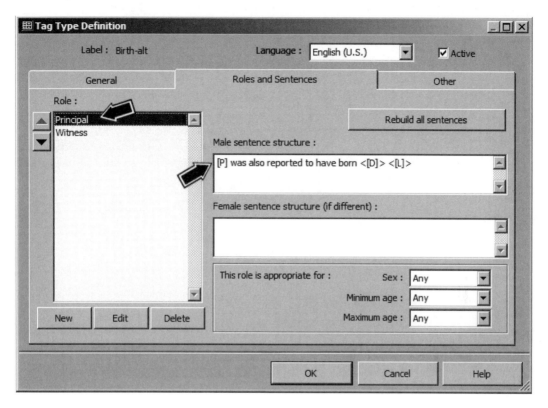

If we wanted to create any custom Roles, we could also create them and add Sentences for them as well. (Custom Roles are discussed in Chapter 13 – Roles.)

Adding a Reminder

We may want to create a "hint" on how to use our custom Tag Type that will appear in the Reminder window when we create a Tag of this type (see page 35). Do that by entering the text of the reminder in the Reminder field on the Other tab of the Report Definition screen, as shown in the screenshot on the following page.

Here we have added a Reminder that we are to enter a Sort Date for our Birth-alt Tags so they will appear after the regular Birth Tags in the Person View and in reports.

The other options on this tab can generally be left at their default settings.

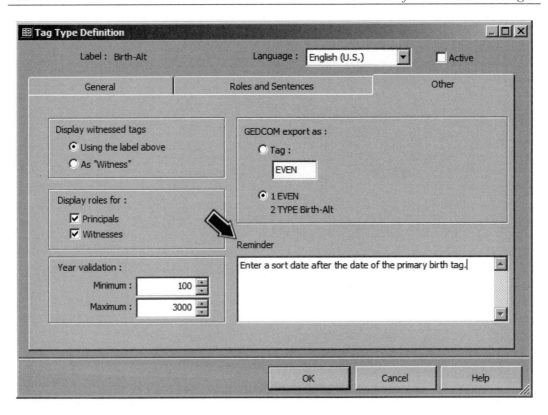

Chapter 15 – Customizing Sources

As we saw in Chapter 6 – Working with Sources, when we enter a Source in TMG we choose a Source Type for that Source. Each Source Type has three output Templates, which tells TMG how to assemble what we enter in the various fields into the first footnote, subsequent footnotes, and the bibliography when we create reports.

Many users find the standard Source Types, with their default Templates, totally adequate. However, some users will want to make minor adjustments in those Templates to better fit their preferences. This chapter provides an introduction to customizing Sources to help readers who want to make such adjustments. Some advanced users prefer to create totally new Source Types and even custom Source Elements. Those subjects are beyond the scope of this guide but are addressed in the resources listed in Appendix A – Other Resources.

In several respects Source Templates are similar to the Sentence Structures discussed in Chapter 9. Both tell TMG how to assemble data we enter into finished text in reports. Sentences do that for Tags, telling TMG how to join the names, dates, place information, and memos into finished narrative text. Source Templates do the same for Sources, telling TMG how to connect data we enter in Sources, Repositories, and Citations into finished footnotes and bibliographies. Both can be modified either locally or globally. They even use somewhat similar styles of coding to tell TMG what to do in the process.

Local vs. Global Source Templates

Source Templates, like Sentence Structures, can be modified in two very different places. You can change them either

> **Globally** – by modifying the Templates of a Source Type. When you do this you are modifying the Templates for every individual Source of that type. Any existing Sources of that type will use the new Template, as will all new Sources of that type you may later create.

> **Locally** – by modifying the Templates for one individual Source. When you do that, you only change that one Source.

> Note: Once you make a change to the local Template of an individual Source, any Global changes made later to the Source Type will *not* have any impact on that individual Source.

Deciding to Modify Templates Locally or Globally

You would generally modify the Source Templates locally if you were going to enter a Source that doesn't quite fit a standard Source Type. For example, if you wanted to create a Source for information from your personal knowledge, you might start with an Interview Source Type. Then, change the phrases "Interview with" and "Interview" in the Templates to something like "Personal knowledge of."

You would more likely want to modify the Templates globally – that is, in the Source Type – if you decide you do not want to use the standard wording of a particular Source Type. For example, in many of the standard Source Types the Full Footnote Template ends with a phrase like this

Hereinafter cited as [ITAL:][SHORT TITLE][:ITAL]

Most style guides suggest that such wording should only be used if the Short Title is so abbreviated as to make it difficult to recognize. So you might delete that entire term from the Templates of your commonly used Source Types.

You might modify the Templates either locally or globally if you decide to create more general sources, with some of the details shifted from the Source Definition to the Citation, as described in the discussion starting on page 29. For example, the Birth Registration (Local Level) Source Type has the following Templates:

Full Footnote: [SUBJECT] entry, [RECORD TYPE]< [NUMBER]><, [CD]>< ([DATE])>, [REPOSITORY], [REPOSITORY ADDRESS].

Short Footnote: [SUBJECT] entry, [RECORD TYPE]< [NUMBER]><, [CD]>< ([DATE])>.

Bibliography: [REPOSITORY ADDRESS]. [RECORD TYPE]. [SUBJECT] entry.

Both the Full and Short Footnotes Templates start with the [SUBJECT] Element, for the name of the person who is the subject of the birth certificate. If you are creating one Source to be used for the birth certificates of several different people, you would want to place the person's name in the Citation Detail. You would then need to either delete the [SUBJECT] Element from the Templates or place it in Conditional Brackets so you do not get the phrase "an unknown person" in your footnotes.

If you plan to create several general Sources of this Type, say one for each county in which you find records, it might be best to make this change globally, in the Source Type. If you expect to make very few, you might choose to make the change locally, in the individual Source.

Where to Modify Source Templates

No matter whether you are adjusting the Template locally for an individual Source or globally for a Source Type, the procedure is the same – the difference is the screen you work with, as described below.

Optional Command
Open Source Types Screen

Source Definition Screen:

Source type

Globally – To modify the Template of a Source Type globally, you open the Edit Source Type Definition screen. To open that screen, you first use the **Tools > Source Types** menu command to open the Source Types List, as shown on the facing page. Select the Source

Type you want to edit from the list. Here we have selected the Census, Federal (Filmed) Source Type.

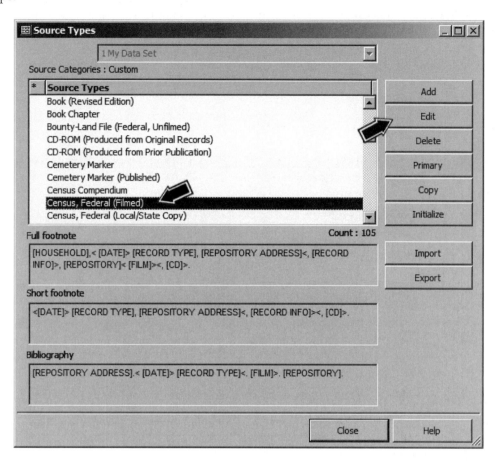

Note that when we select a Source Type the current Templates are displayed in the lower part of the screen. Click the **Edit** button to open the Edit Source Type screen, as shown on the following page.

The Templates for the Full Footnote, Short (subsequent) Footnote, and Bibliography are displayed in the three fields in the center of the screen. You modify the Templates by editing the contents of those fields.

A primer on editing formats is found in the following section, "Editing the Templates."

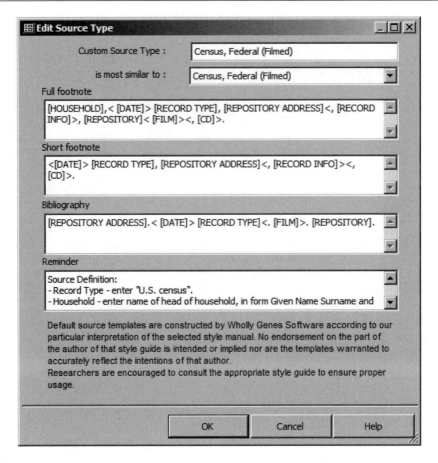

Locally – You modify the Templates locally for an individual Source in the Output Forms tab of the Source Definition screen. You access that screen for an existing Source by selecting the Source in the Master Source List and clicking **Edit**. That is also the screen you access in the course of creating a new Source, as shown in the screenshot on the facing page.

Again we see the three Template fields for the full footnote, short footnote, and bibliography. They will initially be the Templates from the selected Source Type, as seen in the screenshot above.

We can modify the Templates by editing the contents of the three fields.

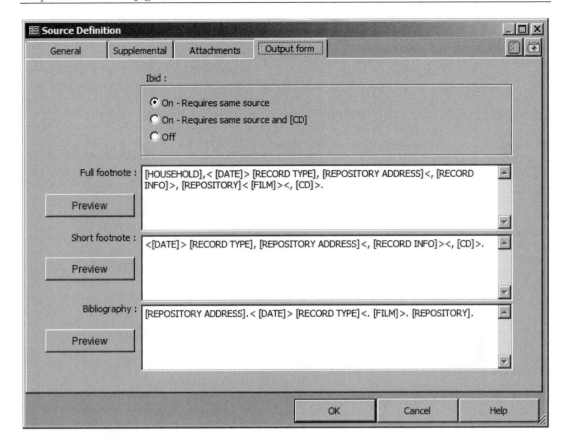

Editing the Templates

Now we look at the specific changes we might make. The first step is to figure out how you want the text in the report to read or exactly how you want to change the existing rendering. Only then can you begin to craft the revised Template itself.

Looking at the existing Template may offer clues. For example, look at the standard Template for the Full Footnote in the Census, Federal (filmed) Source Type, visible in the screenshot above:

> [HOUSEHOLD],< [DATE]> [RECORD TYPE], [REPOSITORY ADDRESS]<, [RECORD INFO]>, [REPOSITORY]< [FILM]><, [CD]>.

The terms in square brackets are **Source Element**s. Source Elements refer to the various fields in the Source Definition, Citation, and Repository Definition screens where the data that will appear in the finished notes is entered. They are conceptually similar to the Variables used in Sentences.

To add an Element to a Template, type the Element name, with the square brackets, in the Template fields. The angle brackets around some Elements – such as "< [DATE]>" in the three templates in the screenshot above – are called Conditional Brackets. They work just as they do in Sentence Structures, telling the program to simply ignore whatever is included between them if the referenced Element is empty. If these brackets are omitted and the indicated Element is empty, a phrase such as "an unknown value" appears in the text in the place of the missing data.

The punctuation marks, like the commas in this example, and any text, will appear in notes exactly as they are written in the Template.

The following screenshot shows the result of a simple change to the global Template for the standard Census, Federal (Filmed) Source Type:

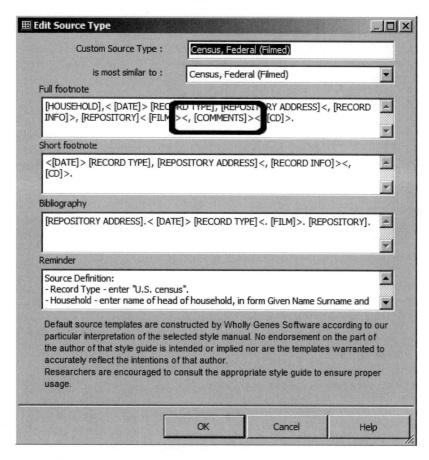

Here the Element [COMMENTS] has been added to the Full Footnote Template, allowing us to record any notes we might want to add. If we viewed the census online instead of on the original microfilm, we might want to say something like "viewed on Ancestry.com," for example.

Note that the new Element has been included in Conditional Brackets, generally a good idea when adding Elements globally.

In the example, a comma and space precede the Element name, inside the Conditional Brackets. If the element is present, the comma and space will be included in the note but will be omitted if the Element is not used.

In this case we want the comment to appear in only the Full Footnote, so we modified only that Template. In other cases, we might want to modify other Templates.

Locations of the Elements

The data input fields for most of the Source Elements appear in the 14 spaces in the center of the General tab of the Source Definition screen. The remainder appear in various other locations, as shown in the following table:

Element	Location
Title	General tab of the Source Definition screen, above the 14 spaces used by the other Elements
Comments	Supplemental tab of the Source Definition screen.
Repository Repository Address Repository Memo	Repository Definition screen, where Repositories are defined.
Repository Reference	Repository Link screen, where Repositories are linked to Sources
CD CM Cref	Citation screen, where Sources are cited for an individual Tag.

Source Elements Are in Groups

If you intend to add an Element to a Source Template, it is important to understand the concept of *Source Element Groups* in TMG, because you cannot use more than one Element of the same Group in any one Source Type or Source. The reason for this is quite obvious once it is understood but seems to be confusing at first, perhaps because the term "Group" is not at all descriptive of the actual process.

What are called "Source Element Groups" actually refer to the physical fields in the data files where the data we enter is stored. It may help to think of them as the "cubbyholes" in an old-fashioned roll-top desk. Each Source we define has 23 of those cubbyholes, each used to store a bit of information about the Source. One might contain the name of the author, another the publisher, and still another the publication date. Each is allowed to contain only one piece of information. Those cubbyholes are what are TMG calls Source Element Groups.

Each Source has its own set of 23 cubbyholes, but they may be used for different items in different Sources. For example, the "author" cubbyhole might contain the name of the informant in an Interview Source or the name of the speaker in a Lecture Source. If TMG used only the Group name, "Author," we would have to remember that the informant's name goes in the cubbyhole labeled "Author" when we create an Interview Source. To avoid this, TMG changes the labels to one appropriate for each Source Type.

The alternate labels for those cubbyholes are called Source Elements in TMG. In any one Source, each cubbyhole can have only one label. You cannot apply two labels and then place two items in the cubbyhole. To translate to TMG's terms, you cannot use two Source Elements in the same Group in a single Source.

Some examples of Elements and their Groups may help. Three of the Groups, and their standard Elements, are listed below:

Group:	Author	Date	Location
Element Names:	Agency	Compile Date	Address
	Author	Date	Author Address
	First Party	File Date	Compiler Address
	Informant	Interview Date	Informant
	Speaker	Printout Date	Address
		Publish Date	Jurisdiction
			Listserve
			Location

How do you know which Elements are in which Groups? Some of the resources listed in Appendix A – Other Resources have lists of them, but the easiest way is to use the **Tools > Source Elements** menu command to open the Source Elements Screen, which is shown on the right. Here we have selected the File Date Element. At the bottom of the screen we can see that this element is in the Date group.

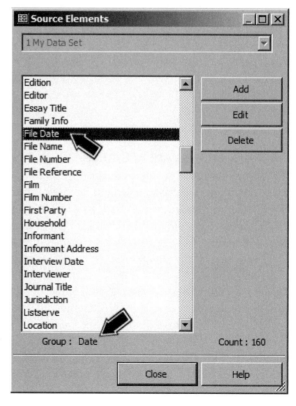

More importantly, how do you figure out which Groups are already in use and which are available? If you are editing an individual Source, the simple way is to click on one of the blank labels in the lower area of the General tab. A Source Elements screen like the one in the screenshot appears, but containing only those elements that are in Groups not already in use in that Source. You can use any of those shown by noting its name and then typing it into the Template.

If you are editing a Source Type, there is no such easy way. The best solution is to open a Source Definition using that Source Type, either an existing Source or a new one. Use the same test of clicking a blank label on the General Tab, noting the name of the desired Element, then return to the Template to type it in.

Groups Designed for Names

Four of the Source Element Groups are designed to be used to record people's names:

- Author
- Editor
- Compiler
- Second Person

They have two special characteristics that are useful for recording names but can cause problems if they are used for other types of data:

- They produce different output for each of the three Templates – the normal given name surname format in the First Footnote; surname only in the Short Footnote; and surname, given name format in the Bibliography. This output depends on entering the names separated by commas and semicolons:
  - For a single person the format is: **Smith, Robert**
  - For multiple people, it is: **Smith, Robert; Jones, Mary; White, Sarah**

- The name of a person in the Data Set can be entered in the Source Element by typing in his or her ID number. The name from that person's Primary Name Tag is then used by the Source Element.

When Source Elements designed for names are used for other types of data, unexpected output will occur if the entry includes either commas or semicolons, or if it begins with a number.

Testing Your Work

When working with Templates, it is always a good idea to test your work with some real data. Local modifications, those made in an individual Source, are easily tested. When you modify the Template of an individual Source, simply use the **Preview** buttons, as described on page 50.

If you make a global change to a Source Type by changing its Template, save your change and then open the Source Definition screen for a Source of the same Type. Use the **Preview** buttons on the Output Form tab of that Source to check the results of your work.

Advanced Topics

This chapter provides only a brief overview of TMG's source recording capabilities. For more information on this subject, consult the sources shown in Appendix A – Other Resources.

Chapter 16 – Projects and Data Sets

TMG has a powerful feature found in few if any other genealogy programs – your data is contained in Projects, each containing one or more Data Sets. Unlike other genealogy programs in which you can only open one Data Set, or "file," at a time, TMG allows you to open, view, and compare multiple Data Sets within a given Project.

If you use only a single Project, don't want to divide your data in any way, and never import data files from another user or found elsewhere, you can ignore the difference between Projects and Data Sets. That means you can ignore this chapter.

But if you want to Import a GEDCOM or other genealogy file (in addition to an Import you might have made to create your initial Project) or if you plan on creating separate subsets of your data, it is important that you understand these terms and how Projects and Data Sets relate to each other. This chapter explains what they are, how they differ, and discusses some issues that arise when working with them.

What is a Data Set?

A **Data Set** contains information about a group of people. It is what users commonly think of as a "file" in most genealogy programs. In TMG, Data Sets cannot exist by themselves. They are always contained within a Project.

A Data Set

The important concept is that everyone in the Data Set can

- Be linked to each other by parent/child links or by marriage.

- Appear as Witnesses in each others' event Tags.

- Be included in reports, charts, and forms with each other.

- Be cited in the same set of Sources.

- Have access to the same set of standard or customized Tag Types and Source Types.

A Data Set can contain any number of people, who may or may not be related to each other.

Most users find it most convenient to keep everyone in a single Data Set, because the points above then apply to everyone in their data.

So then What is a Project?

A **Project** is a group of Data Sets that you open at one time in TMG.

When you have more than one Data Set in a Project, you can

- Use the Project Explorer, Picklist, or Check for Duplicate People function to search for people in different Data Sets who may be duplicates or related to each other.

- Compare information on the same person who may appear in more than one Data Set.

- Copy or move people from one Data Set to another.

Project with 1 Data Set

Most of the time users work with Projects containing only one Data Set.

Project with 2 Data Sets

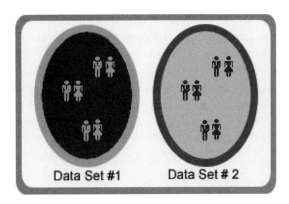

Data Set #1   Data Set # 2

You might want a second Data Set in a Project to compare them, or to copy people from one to the other.

But the Data Sets remain independent, which means you cannot

- Link as parent and child or as spouses a person in one Data Set to a person in another Data Set.

- Cite a Source in one Data Set in a Tag in another Data Set.

- Use Tag Types or Source Types modified or created in one Data Set in another Data Set.

- Merge two copies of the same person when you find the same person appearing in two different Data Sets.

Data Sets may be added or deleted from a Project at any time, or they can be temporarily "Disabled" so they do not appear to be part of the Project. See page 142 for details.

Maybe an Analogy Would Help

If the descriptions above don't clarify how Projects and Data Sets are related, perhaps a simple analogy would help. It's not a perfect analogy by any means, but it does illustrate some useful aspects of the Projects/Data Sets concept.

Imagine that a Data Set is represented by a family tree diagram drawn on a transparent film, like a slide for an overhead projector. The diagram will depict relationships, show names, and maybe show some events with dates and places. There may even be footnotes with source information on the slide.

Next, let's say you have one Data Set (slide) for your family. Then you receive a file from a distant cousin, and you expect some of the people in your Data Set will also be on the file you received. You import that file into your Project, where it becomes a second Data Set – a second slide – showing the tree prepared by your cousin.

Put one slide over the other, and move them around looking for places where some of the same people are shown. Slide them around this way and that until you find bits that are the same. Then you can compare the information in the two Data Sets (slides) to see if there is anything new in the data from your cousin.

This is a very basic idea of what you can do with two Data Sets in a single Project in TMG. Note that the two sets of data (the slides) stay separate. You can compare them, reading part from one and then the other. But they never connect with each other; they always remain completely separate. Even such aspects as the source notes always remain separate. There is no linkage between the notes on one slide and those on the other.

There is one important aspect of using Data Sets in TMG that isn't apparent from this analogy. While TMG keeps the two Data Sets separate, you can copy or move parts of the data from one Data Set to the other or merge them entirely as described in the following sections.

Why Use More than One Data Set or Project?

Most users will find Projects with just a single Data Set meet their needs most of the time. There are a few cases where separate Data Sets are useful:

- When you Import a GEDCOM file, a file from another program, or a Data Set from an earlier version of TMG, TMG always places the imported information in a new Data Set. If you have TMG place this new Data Set in your existing Project, you can take advantage of all the features to compare the information in the new data with what you already have. You can then copy specific information, copy people or groups of people, or merge the entire Data Set with your existing one. Or you may want to simply delete the new Data Set after examining it.

- Those who work with the data of others, such as professionals and those who keep records of family associations, will likely want to keep separate Projects.

Those who wish to maintain separate Data Sets have to decide whether it is best to keep them in the same Project or create separate Projects. Keeping them in the same Project makes it easy to switch from viewing one to another. If you should find the people in one are related to those in the other, you can copy parts of one Data Set to the other. If keeping them together creates such a large Project that performance is unacceptable, dividing into separate Projects may be helpful. Few users have Data Sets large enough for this to be a concern.

Data Sets and ID Numbers

When you have more than one Data Set in a Project, TMG adds the Data Set number in front of the ID numbers assigned to each person and in front of such things as Source numbers so you can distinguish which ones belong to which Data Set. So the people in your first Data Set will have ID numbers like 1:1, 1:2, 1:3, etc., while those in your second Data Set will be numbered 2:1, 2:2, 2:3, and so on. The following view of the Picklist in a Project with two Data Sets may make this more clear:

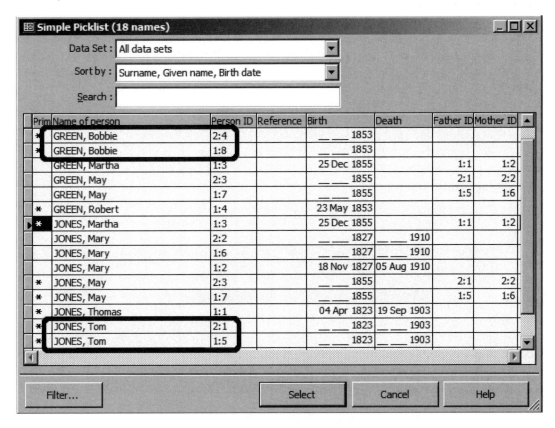

We can see that each ID Number is prefixed with the Data Set number. This example is a Project in which we have imported data from a cousin that contains some of the same people already in our own data. There are several cases where apparently the same person appears in both Data Sets, which we can distinguish by noting the Data Set numbers.

"Switching" Data Sets

Users sometimes ask how they "switch" between the Data Sets in a Project that contains more than one Data Set. The short answer is you don't!

Rather, you just navigate to the desired person, regardless of which Data Set that person may be in. You choose a person from the Picklist, Project Explorer, by ID Number, or most of the other methods available to move from one person to another. (The only one you can't use is to double-click on the name in the Details, Children, Siblings, or Associates windows, because those windows can only include people in a single Data Set.)

Screens such as Master Place List, Master Source List, etc., generally have filters at the top that allow you to see items from only one Data Set if you like.

When you add a new person, by default that person is added in the same Data Set as the current focus person in the Details screen. If you start the add person process by clicking on the Add Person Toolbar button or using the **Add > Add person** menu command, there is a drop-down list at the top of the Add Person Type screen that allows you to select a different Data Set if you choose.

There is one way, sort of, to "switch" Data Sets. You can Disable one or more Data Sets, and the people in them will not appear on any lists, nor will places, sources, etc., appear on those lists. This may be useful if you want to only view one Data Set and hide all the others. You Disable or Enable Data Sets with the Data Set Manager.

Managing Data Sets

The main tool used to manage Data Sets within a single Project is the Data Set Manager:

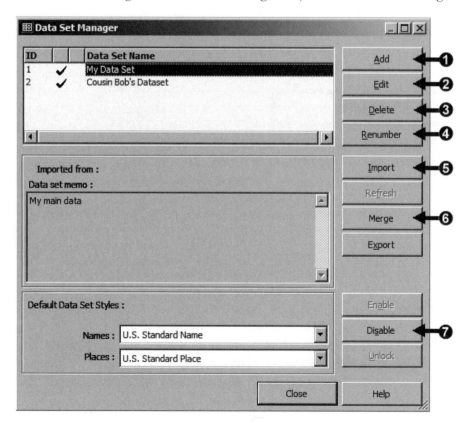

The most commonly used functions in the Data Set Manager are

❶ Add – used to add a new, empty, Data Set in which you can enter people.

❷ Edit – allows you to edit the name or memo of the selected Data Set. The memo is an optional note about the contents or origin of the Data Set.

❸ Delete – removes the selected Data Set. You might use this when you are finished examining imported data and no longer want to keep it in your Project.

❹ Renumber – allows you to change the Data Set ID numbers.

❺ Import – used to import data; the same function as the **File > Import** menu command.

❻ Merge – combines two Data Sets. See the following sections for details.

❼ Disable – with the companion **Enable** button, will make the selected Data Set visible or invisible while working in the Project. This is useful to temporarily remove the clutter of multiple Data Sets while still keeping them in the Project.

Another tool used to manage Data Sets is the List of People report. It can be used to copy selected people in a Data Set to a new a Data Set or Project. See page 72 for details.

About Merging Projects and Data Sets

You can merge two Projects so the combined Project then contains all the Data Sets from both Projects. You can also merge two Data Sets in a Project so that the people in both are then in a single Data Set.

Before we look at the mechanics of the individual processes, we should take note of one point that sometimes leaves users confused. The term "merge" leads one to expect that two Projects or Data Sets will become one. That is not actually what happens. Rather, the contents of one is copied, or appended, to the other. The first does not disappear, but remains unchanged.

Thus after "merging" two Projects, we still have two projects, one of which includes the Data Sets formerly in the other in addition to those it originally contained. Likewise, after "merging" two Data Sets in a Project, we still see two Data Sets, but one includes the people formerly in the other in addition to those previously in it. If we really want to have only one Project or Data Set, we then have to delete the one that still has only its original contents.

We can control which Project or Data Set will contain the combined results and which will remain unchanged from the Merge screen. The Merge Projects screen, shown in the screenshot on the following page, illustrates the process.

After entering the two Projects to be Merged, we look at the box in the lower half of the screen and select one of the two options there. For me, reading the explanation in parentheses is the key. The first one, selected here, says "Project B remains intact." That is, it is not changed. So, Project A is the one that will end up after the Merge containing the contents formerly in both projects. The wording is slightly different on the Merge Data Sets screen, but the meaning is the same.

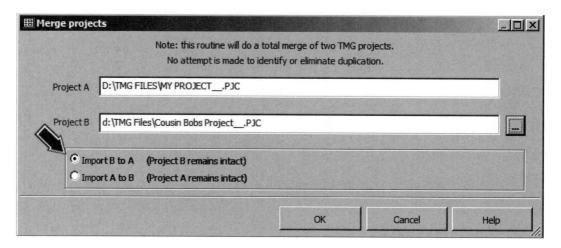

The main significance of choosing the order of the Merge is to determine how the individual Data Sets or People are numbered. The Project that ends up with the combined results will have its original Data Set(s) numbered first, with those copied from the other Project being assigned higher numbers. Likewise, when two Data Sets are Merged, the one with the combined results will have its original people, Sources, and Repositories assigned to their original numbers, with those from the other Data Set being assigned higher numbers.

Merging Projects

The mechanics of Merging two Projects are straightforward:

1. Open one of the Projects then use the **File > Merge Projects** menu command to open the Merge Projects screen, as shown above.
2. Enter the second Project, either by typing in the location and name or by clicking the [...] button to the right of the field for the name and locating it.
3. Make the desired selection in the box in the lower part of the screen.
4. Click **OK**.

That is all that's required. If you want to now Merge the Data Sets in the combined Project, proceed as described in the next section.

Merging Data Sets

The mechanics of Merging Data Sets are similar to that of Merging Projects. Starting with the Project that contains the two Data Sets open, you then

1. Use the **File > Data Set Manager** menu command to open the Data Set Manger.

2. Select one of the Data Sets you want to Merge, and click the **Merge** button to open the Merge Data Set screen, which is similar to the one on the facing page for Merging Projects.

3. Select the second Data Set from the drop-down list.

4. Make the desired selection in the box in the lower part of the screen.

5. Click **OK**.

If the two Data Sets contained some of the same people, each of those people will appear twice in the combined Data Set. They can be combined by using the **Tools > Merge Two People** menu command to open the Merge Two People screen. After you select the two people to be merged, click **OK** to see a side-by-side display of the two people with all their Tags listed. You can select which Tags from each person will be kept for the combined person. After merging, all the Tags previously attached to both people will be attached to the combined person unless some were unchecked in the Split Display. So there could well be two Name Tags with the same name, and duplicates of Relationship and various event Tags. The two Tags of each pair should be checked for information or citations not contained in the other, and then generally one of them would be deleted.

Because Merging Data Sets requires actually combining a long list of elements, including Tag Types, Source Types, Flags and more, there are several issues that can arise. Addressing them is beyond the scope of this guide, but they are addressed in some of the resources listed in Appendix A – Other Resources.

Using Copy Persons Rather than Merging Data Sets

If you merge two Data Sets that contain a lot of the same people, you end up with the problem of having a lot of duplicate people to merge, one by one. You may want to include only a few of the people from the second Data Set. If so, consider using the Copy Person(s) function instead of merging the entire Data Sets. It allows you to copy only the desired people from one Data Set to the other.

It is important to copy as many people as possible in a single operation, rather than one at a time. When people are copied individually, all the Tags that contain two Principals are copied without the second Principal. Therefore, all parent/child links are broken, Marriage Tags no longer indicate who the spouse is, and all events with two principals will only indicate one of them. Witnessed events are not copied at all unless one of the Principals is copied at the same time.

There are two ways to select the people to be copied. You can select them in the Project Explorer or collect them in a Focus Group (see page 22). In general, using the Focus Group method is simpler and less error prone. After you have all the desired people selected, use the **Add > Copy Person(s)** menu command to open the Copy Person screen. In the lower half of that screen, choose the Focus Group or Project Explorer depending on which method you used to select the group. Specify which Data Set the people are to be copied into. You can choose the types of data to be copied on the Data Types to Include tab if you like. Click **OK** to complete the copy operation.

Appendix A – Other Resources

This guide, focusing on helping new users become comfortable with TMG, is necessarily limited in scope. TMG has many features not covered, and many of the features discussed have aspects that are not covered. Further, with a program as flexible as TMG, there are many ways to accomplish a given task. Exchanges with other users can suggest methods that might better serve your preferences and objectives. For additional information about the use of TMG, I suggest the following:

- **Help** – is probably the first resource to consult. TMG has a well-written Help function with a great deal of depth in describing how each feature works. For assistance with a particular feature, click the **Help** button that is present in most screens, or press F1.

- **Wholly Genes Support Forum** – is the official support forum for TMG, where you can post questions and receive responses from Wholly Genes staff and other users. Access it by going to the Wholly Genes website at www.whollygenes.com and choosing Support Forum from the Support menu at the top of the page.

- **TMG List on RootsWeb** – is an e-mail list for users of TMG to discuss any subject related to use of TMG. This seems to be the best place for questions about the "best way" to do anything in TMG. The List archives can be searched at archiver.rootsweb.com – enter "TMG" in the box for the name of the list.

  Subscribe to the List at: lists.rootsweb.com/index/other/Software/TMG.html

- **Terry's TMG Tips** – is my website, available online at: tmg.reigelridge.com

- **Lee Hoffman's TMG Tips** – is available online at: www.tmgtips.com

- **Caroline Gurney's TMG pages** – are of particular interest to users with interests in the United Kingdom, but some articles are useful to everyone. Online at: gurney.pwp.blueyonder.co.uk/TMG.htm

- *Getting the Most Out of The Master Genealogist* – the book edited by Lee Hoffman, with chapters authored by many experienced TMG users, including the author of this guide. It covers many topics in more depth than this volume, including many more advanced topics. It is available at the Wholly Genes web store.

- **Local TMG User Groups** – are established in many communities. To see if there is one near you, check the "Other Resources" section of the Wholly Genes Support Forum, and under that the section look for "User Groups."

- **Corrections to this Guide** – including those related to features added to TMG after the guide went to press, are available on the update page on my website: tmg.reigelridge.com/primer

Appendix B – Shortcut Keys

Users who prefer to work from the keyboard rather than the mouse may find the following list of shortcut keys helpful:

Data Entry

Key	Function	Key	Function
F2	Search (see page 41)	Ctrl+V	Add Name Variation Tag
F3	Repeat (see page 41)	Ctrl+B	Add Birth Tag
Ctrl+F3	Repeat list (see page 41)	Ctrl+M	Add Marriage Tag
F4	Add Tag, Citation, Source, Repository	Ctrl+D	Add Death Tag
		Ctrl+U	Add Burial Tag
F5	Edit Tag, Citation, Source, Repository	Ctrl+C	Copy
F6	Delete Tag, Citation, Source, Repository	Ctrl+V	Paste
		Delete	Delete
F7	Enlarge Memo field	Esc	Cancel
F9	OK, Close, or Select	Enter	Open selected Tag, Witness, or Citation

Navigation

Key	Function	Key	Function
F1	Open Help	Ctrl+T	Open Tree View
Ctrl+A	Open Accent Definition screen	Ctrl+L	Return to previous focus person
Ctrl+K	Open Bookmark Manager	Ctrl+I	New focus person by ID Number
Ctrl+R	Open Relationship Calculator		
Ctrl+P	Open Person View	Ctrl+Enter	Change focus to selected person
Ctrl+Y	Open Family View		

Index